To Carol + Bob —
Best wishes to.
to Two fine "Go
Dike Zoo
Diana Lenz

M000239601

DIKE EDDLEMAN

Illinois' Greatest Athlete

DIANA EDDLEMAN LENZI

SPORTS PUBLISHING INC.
a division of Sagamore Publishing
Champaign, IL 61820

©1997 Diana Eddleman Lenzi
All rights reserved.

Editor: Richard Barak
Director of Production: Susan M. McKinney
Book design: Michelle R. Dressen
Dustjacket design: Julie L. Denzer

ISBN:1-57167-199-4

Printed in the United States

SPORTS PUBLISHING INC.
804 N. Neil
Champaign IL 61820
www.sagamorepub.com

*This book is dedicated to Teddy Eddleman,
the antithesis of the "little woman," who has
been a loving wife, mother and cheerleader
for the entire Eddleman team.*

*And—to all loyal Illini everywhere—
Oskee-Wow-Wow Illinois!*

———————————————

TABLE OF CONTENTS

FOREWORD

The Fighting Illini sports "family" encompasses an impressive list. Among the names, one stands apart. Dike Eddleman, Illinois' greatest all-around athlete, is a friend to many, a stranger to none, and admired by all.

Growing up in the '50s and '60s, Dike Eddleman was one of those sport names consistently discussed with my friends. He represented not only athletic achievement, but was a terrific role model. Working with him through the years, I have discovered his unselfish attitude and his love for people are his greatest attributes. After reading his biography, I think you will agree.

I am proud to include Dike's name at the top of the University of Illinois roster of outstanding athletes. As I look back on the great heritage that shaped the Fighting Illini sports program, Dike looms larger than life, not only for his athletic achievements, but for his loyalty, integrity and dedication.

Dike's purpose at Illinois has been to promote a university that became his second home. Standing on the threshold of a new century, remembering Dike's contributions will encourage future excellence.

Although new sports heroes replace the old, one name has endured. Thanks to his daughter, Diana, the story of Dike and the Eddleman years will remain a rich part of Illinois' colorful history.

Ronald Guenther
Director of Athletics
University of Illinois

A LETTER FROM DIKE

Dear friends,

Athletics have made my life a continuous drama filled with hopes, dreams, frustration, excitement, disappointment and comedy. As I reflect on my 70-plus years, I can honestly say I have been a very lucky man who has lived a full and happy life. Through the years, I have been richly blessed with a wonderful family, faithful friends and loyal fans.

Centralia, Illinois, holds a special place in my heart because it was in my hometown that Teddy and I started our exciting life together. The University of Illinois, one of the world's finest educational institutions, is and will remain a unique haven of glorious memories for us as you will discover.

Although it seems with the passing of time that I run faster, jump higher and punt the ball farther, my daughter, Diana, has written an accurate, chronological account of my life and athletic achievements. For those of you who are my age or older, I invite you to relive some memorable moments. For those of younger generations, I hope you enjoy the sports history you will discover from my era.

As the events of my life are recounted, I can't help but remember those who taught me how to care for others, develop my talents and adopt unselfish commitments. To those who positively guided and influenced my life, I will be eternally grateful.

Remembering the past has been a powerful experience. As I wandered down memory lane, Tennyson's poem "Ulysses" came to mind—the last six lines in particular:

"Tho' much is taken, much abides; and tho'
We are not now that strength which in old days
Moved earth and heaven, that which we are, we are
One equal temper of heroic hearts,
Made weak by time and fate, but strong in will
To strive, to seek, to find, and not to yield."

My high school coach, Arthur L. Trout, impressed upon me the importance of team building. My success in athletics and in life was the result of the team spirit shared by fellow players, family, friends and fans. It is with a great deal of gratitude, affection and sadness that I remember those teachers, coaches, players and friends who are no longer with us but who played a vital role in my life story. Their presence and friendship are greatly missed. I mourn the loss of these individuals, the likes of whom will never be seen again.

I remember ... Fred Corray, Champaign-Urbana radio announcer and great sports historian; Fred Pearson, a fabulous guard on the Orphan team who spent his life dedicated to teaching basketball to the youth of Centralia; Farrell Robinson, the Orphan who single-handedly won the sectional tournament game in 1942, allowing us to advance to the state tournament finals; Bill Butler, my close friend and confidant from Bloomington, who so dearly loved Illinois athletics. And I will never forget all the great coaches ... Bob McCall, Harry Lutz, Arthur Trout, Ray Eliot, Leo Johnson, Harry Combes and Dr. Harold Osborn. The list of high-caliber individuals who influenced my life goes on and on.

With their passing, we have lost the opportunity for reminiscing, for counseling, for companionship. Gone is the opportunity to share a laugh or to shed a tear. As I look back, I see that "much is taken," and we are diminished because of it. However, I believe that makes this book even more significant. Sharing my story gives validity to Tennyson's words "much abides." The people mentioned in this book have made a positive contribution to society, and, through this, their influence remains.

The mere mention of names such as Zuppke, Grange and Huff evoke timeless memories because of their contributions to the sports world. They are not remembered for a winning season or one great play, but for elevating the level of sports consciousness for all men. Their contributions were neither self-serving nor self-centered. And, perhaps, that is the message I hope is conveyed in this book: to lead a purposeful life utilizing your talents to meet your own needs in a way that will help others. We must feel compassion for others and react to that feeling.

Whether you are an athlete or a sports fanatic, you should discover and develop your strengths, always striving for academic excellence. As Tennyson reminds us, our physical strengths will be "made weak by time and fate." But it is our desire and spirit that will endure. Live life with a heroic heart and the will to win. When life gets tough, don't be a quitter. Strive toward your goals and never lose sight of your commitments.

From my years of experience as a team player, my best advice is never be afraid to contribute. When you give from the heart, no contribution is ever too small.

Go Illini!
Dike Eddleman
Bielfeldt Athletic Building
1700 South Fourth Street
Champaign, IL 61820

ACKNOWLEDGMENTS

The biography of this singular athlete has been written with the help of many individuals whose lives have been touched by this extraordinary man. A debt of gratitude is owed to the many family members, friends, fans and teammates who shared their memories so the legacy of my father's contributions to sports could be preserved accurately.

Although this book has been a labor of love, the most difficult part was getting the "man" to talk about his accomplishments. True to character, he remains modest—almost to a fault. But thank you, Dad, for reliving all those special moments with me. I hope your story will inspire athletes everywhere for you are one-in-a-million. As Dike's "adoring daughter," I have tried to tell this story objectively. Please excuse any weak moments when a daughter's love for her parents might have surfaced. I plead guilty to having two of the best! Sharing their story has been a privilege and a pleasure.

Although the most enjoyable research for this book was listening to my father reminisce, I have gained invaluable assistance from a multitude of friends and acquaintances whom I wish to thank. First and foremost, I want to thank my mother for her excellent memory and the firsthand accounts of her life with Dad.

The person who planted the seed for the idea of writing a book about my father was Dr. Kevin Lasley, one of my graduate school professors at Eastern Illinois University. He has been a source of inspiration and encouragement. I also want to recognize Dr. Scott Crawford, my graduate adviser and friend. Two better mentors can't be found.

There were numerous individuals who answered my letters and requests for interviews. Dr. George Ross, historian for Marion County in Sandoval, Illinois, taught me about Centralia's history. His knowledge of Dad's early years proved insightful. Another person who convinced me this was a viable project was Bill Davies. A lifelong friend and teammate of my father's, he made a cassette tape that I will keep for posterity. Making new friends was one of the most enjoyable aspects of my research. I had the pleasure of sharing some warm moments with Arthur Trout's daughter, Pat Nardelli, of San Diego. Randy List, former sports editor of the *Centralia Sentinel*, provided me with my first interview. I enjoyed the letters and poems that I received from Merle Rogers, Flip Seely and Bill Lindenberg. Part of my Southern Illinois "team" included Chuck Holt, who provided photographs for the book. In Salem, Illinois, I spent several hours with Bob Roddy, whose investigative efforts helped produce grade school pictures of Dad.

I would like to thank the Rev. Bob Richards for his recap of the 1948 Olympic experience. Pat Harmon, historian/curator of the National Football Foundation's College Hall of Fame, sent pages of interesting facts. Although Seely Johnston is in his 90s, he is one of the youngest at heart and most knowledgeable sports historians I have known. A special friend of my father's, he is one-of-a-kind whose recollections of University of Illinois athletics is tempered with wisdom. The late Fred Corray, the voice of the Fighting Illini during the Eddleman era, was extremely sharp on sports details. I always will remember the sincerity of his words.

I would like to thank University of Illinois Athletic Director Ron Guenther for his cooperation and promotion of my efforts. Mike Pearson of Sagamore Publishing and Dave Johnson from the U. of I. Sports Information Office were generous in sharing files and expertise. This book would not have been possible without Teresa Bertram's computer skills. Louita Hartwell, Dad's loyal and efficient secretary, gave wonderful assistance. Then there are the three Lous: Lou Henson, Lou Tepper and Lou Boudreau. Gene Vance's recollection of the Whiz Kids and early professional basketball years was enlightening. Thanks to all the true blue Illini who contributed!

My parents' neighbors and friends from Gibson City made my hometown a special place. Life seemed so safe and secure while I was growing up there. Friends like the Dick Walter family and Dick Moody come along only once in a lifetime. Thanks for all the memories.

Residing only 20 miles south of Champaign-Urbana in Tuscola, Illinois, are several Illini who helped shed light on this subject. Bill Huber, former football standout who played on Ray Eliot's 1947 Rose Bowl team, helped clarify the postwar years. Bill Butkovich, former Illini football and baseball player, recalled the days when the annual golf outings began in Douglas County with the help of Bill McCarty and Red Proffitt.

Now that Dike has returned to the university as a consultant for the Fighting Illini Scholarship Fund, he looks forward to spending some time with members of his extended "Illini family" such as Will and Marty Thomson, Ed and Matti Schmidt, Edie and Bob Lane, Bill and Marilyn Hopper, Tim and Connie McCallister, Charlene Cain, Sharon Wade and Cal Hugy. Thanks to all of you for the great stories. May the good times continue!

To Gene Lenzi, the love of my life, I give special thanks for believing in my dreams and making them come true. Let's never lose the magic!

Diana E. Lenzi

INTRODUCTION

Heroes. We all search for them, those special people whose aspirations have taken them to a higher plateau for deeds performed with courage and conviction. Many times, those we call "hero" are athletes. The story I want to share with you is about my Dad, Thomas Dwight "Dike" Eddleman, a living legend in Illinois sports and the personification of the heroic figure.

His athletic achievements will take you back to a simpler time when the world seemed more positive and moral, life seemed less complicated and crude, and athletes played for the love of the sport instead of outrageous salaries and incredible endorsements.

Unlike many modern sports heroes, Eddleman's life story does not include tales of violence, corruption or sexual exploitation. It focuses on the development of ethics and character. His life becomes living testimony that an emphasis on the fundamentals of sports contributes to a winning attitude and exemplary sportsmanship.

Recalling Dike's lifetime of athletic adventures, it becomes clear why Dad is referred to as the greatest all-around athlete in Illinois' history. Possessing a tremendous natural ability and drive, his athletic pursuits resulted in outstanding performances in three major sports.

After beginning his football career at Centralia High School, Dad continued his success at the University of Illinois, where he played on the 1947 Rose Bowl team. He holds the university's season punting record, a 43-yard average, and the record for the longest punt, an 88-yarder.

His basketball achievements include a stellar performance in the 1942 Illinois State High School Basketball championship game, when the Orphans captured Centralia's third state tournament title for renowned prep coach Arthur L. Trout. Centralia participated in the state tournament three out of Dad's four years in high school. After a successful basketball career at the University of Illinois, which included a trip to the Final Four, my father played professional basketball for the Tri-City Blackhawks, the Milwaukee Hawks (forerunners of the Atlanta Hawks), and the Fort Wayne Zollner Pistons (forerunners of the Detroit Pistons).

A sensational track career of sprinting, long-jumping and high-jumping culminated in a trip to the 1948 Olympics in London. There, Dad participated as a high jumper on the United States track team, coming home with a medal.

Dad's diversity in athletic achievements remains unequaled. He is the only athlete at the University of Illinois to have earned 11 varsity letters.

PREFACE

Even at his birth on December 27, 1922, Thomas Dwight "Dike" Eddleman proved he was unusual. Dike, born to German-English parents, experienced health problems at birth and suffered a negative reaction to the milk he was fed. Family physician Dr. Henry Kissle treated him with a black salve and ordered him to be kept wrapped tightly in a blanket. Several nourishments were tried until, finally, the newborn responded to goat's milk, which was provided by a neighbor. Dike's determination and tenacity at birth might be viewed as an omen.

Dike's father, Thomas Edward Eddleman, and his father's second wife, Alma Marie (Snider), lived in Centralia, Illinois, when their only son was born two days after Christmas in the front bedroom of their home at 226 N. Maple St. The baby had a sister, Josephine, and two half-sisters, Dorothy and LaVonne. Unfortunately, Dike never had a chance to know his mother because she died of pneumonia when he was only two years old. Dorothy Root, Dike's oldest sibling, recalled: "I remember my brother when he was only two years old going to the window, holding a picture of his mother and crying. It just broke your heart to see him so sad."

Despite Dike's troubled entrance into the world, fate had smiled upon this Southern Illinois lad, who was born a gifted athlete. Possessing charisma and exceptional athletic talent, he developed a superlative sports career during a simpler time that will be remembered in Illinois as the Eddleman Era.

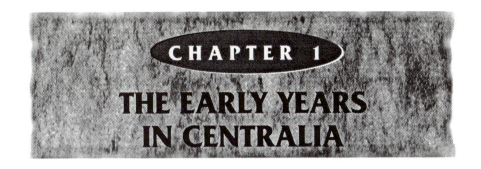

CHAPTER 1

THE EARLY YEARS IN CENTRALIA

 As long as I can remember, I've called my favorite athlete "Dad." A tall, virile man, my father has a sensitivity and tenderness about him that makes him unique from other sports personalities. As a child, I was mesmerized by his lucid blue eyes, his dazzling smile and his magnificent hugs, which kept me safe from any misfortune that came my way. Now that I have a family, my children look to him for that same strength and compassion. Long before I knew about his athletic prowess, Dike Eddleman was my hero.

A country boy who made it to the big leagues, my father never let his fame alter his ego. To better understand his success, it is necessary to begin in a place called Perks in Southern Illinois. Although he was born and reared in Centralia, Illinois, his grandparents lived in the rural town of Dongola, which consisted of a general store, a gas station and a country school. It was 10 miles from Dongola—in Perks—where Dike spent many childhood summers on his Aunt Laura's farm. Aunt Laura was Dike's father's sister-in-law.

"I have vivid memories of summers spent on the family farm. You've never really felt hot until you've lived through a Southern

Illinois summer without air conditioning," Dike recalled about his life in the early 1930s. "I remember working with a farmhand named Patches, harvesting wheat for my aunt and uncle."

The hard physical labor helped Dike develop his upper body strength. "For as long as I can remember, I was told that hard work was good for the body as well as the soul. Working up a sweat has always seemed to have a cleansing effect on me. To this day, I love to work outdoors, close to nature." Dike's daily chores whetted his appetite. "Our days would start at sunrise. By 11 a.m., we'd be ravenous! My aunt would ring a large bell and call us to lunch. Everything was fresh—the eggs had been gathered that morning; there was homemade bread still warm from the oven; there were freshly smoked hams and sausage from my uncle's own smokehouse; and for dessert, my aunt would serve these really tall angel food cakes with homemade ice cream. We'd eat so much that we would all have to take an hour nap before we went back to work. There wasn't much to do at night but gather around the radio or talk with friends. It was early to bed because we would wake up with the chickens the next morning."

While visiting his grandparents in Dongola, Dike saw an athletic uniform hanging in the closet. "It belonged to my Uncle Van, and I remember asking my Grandmother Snider if I could have it."

Before long, Dike's wish to wear an athletic uniform would come true. During his ensuing athletic career, he would don many uniforms.

Although Dike enjoyed summers and vacations on the farm, he spent most of his time in Centralia, where his father, Tom Eddleman, worked for the Illinois Central Railroad. Dike's birthplace was a thriving miniature metropolis made up of railroaders, coal miners, farmers and businessmen. Centralia began to flourish in the 1850s when the Illinois Central railroad line was constructed. It was followed by the Southern, C. B. & Q., and M.

& I. lines. The railroads influenced the city's economy. By the 1930s, they employed a quarter of Centralia's 17,000 people.

The railroad's wood-burning engines eventually were converted into coal-burners. Centralia was a perfect source for this natural resource, and, as a result, coal mines were sunk, attracting many Irish, Italian and German workers. The rail lines' development attracted many industries. Others settled in Southern Illinois because of the fruit crops that flourished there. Strawberry patches, along with apple, pear, cherry and peach orchards, thrived under the skilled hands of local farmers.

The town was proud of its Peach Festivals, May fetes and Halloween celebrations. Just as important as these annual events was the town's passion for athletics. People were drawn to any kind of athletic competition, especially football, basketball, baseball and boxing. By the 1940s, the coal mines, orchards and oil fields had boosted the economy, causing Centralia to become a boom town. Townspeople, many of whom became wealthy overnight, often appeared to have plenty of money for a drink and a friendly wager on sporting events. Such events were a recreational outlet for these hard-working citizens.

Caught up in this spirit, Dike exhibited an early enthusiasm for athletics. His sister, Josephine Brosnan, said her younger brother had a ball in his hands as far back as she can remember. Raymond Root, a brother-in-law, had nailed a hoop to a neighbor's barn. Josephine said, "If we ever wanted to find Dwight, we knew just where to look."

Dike began playing sports when he was 5 or 6 with neighborhood friends. "I was taller and stronger than other boys my age. The older kids were always forming teams for baseball or basketball. It really felt great when the older boys asked me to play with them."

Eddleman's father, who possessed a strapping, athletic physique, traveled as a conductor for the Illinois Central Railroad from age 16. Tom Eddleman's job caused him to be away from home. Consequently, Dike had little male guidance or discipline during his youth. "My Dad was gone for days at a time. I remember being very excited whenever he returned home from a trip. When I was in grade school, the trains still had steam engines. I remember the noise and the smells as the trains pulled into town. I would often run out to the water tower and wait for the flagmen to stop the train. I'd hop on and ride the train those few blocks into the station. It was such an exciting experience for a young boy. The greatest highlight of these trips would be my father allowing me to carry his railroad lantern for him as we walked home. I also remember my Dad stopping by Louie Diepert's grocery store to pay our bill. I looked forward to that because I'd always get a small bag of candy. One of the benefits of my Dad's job on the railroad was getting free passes. I took advantage of those free rides many times throughout my life. Sometimes my family would ride the Illinois Central to Dongola just to have lunch with my relatives."

Dike found lots of neighborhood boys to pal around with while growing up on Maple Street in Centralia. He would play outside from dawn to dusk with such friends as Bill Davies, Bob Roddy, Philip Seely, Farrell Robinson, Russell Ditterline, Bill Salisbury, and Paul and Clifton Lynn. "We'd play together all the time. We loved to shoot baskets. We also built a high-jump pit in Stanley Egger's back yard. In the mid-1930s, there was a great athlete from Centralia named Lowell Spurgeon, who excelled as a high jumper. We would all pretend we were Spurgeon and jump over our bamboo pole," Bill Davies said.

Philip Seely, better known as "Flip," laughed about an incident that he and Bob Boston remember: "Just like all young boys, Dike could be mischievous. The Eddlemans lived one block away from Saint Mary's Catholic Church. One Sunday morning, Dike hopped on a tricycle with a young female companion named Mary Meagher. The two of them proceeded to ride right down the center aisle of that church during high Mass. Needless to say, it caused quite a commotion."

Bob Roddy recalled the many trips the boys took to the reservoir. "During those hot Centralia summers, we'd all walk or hitchhike out to the levy to cool off. The problem was—I couldn't swim. One day, Dike said, 'The best way to learn is by doing.' With that, he threw me into the water and quickly had to pull me out before I drowned. Believe it or not, he taught me how to swim that summer. Dike has a great deal of patience, and he has always liked helping people."

Eddleman attended Central Grade School. During his elementary years, Eddleman was an average student. "One day I remember being punished. Mrs. Martha Watson put me in the 'blue room' and locked the door. Unfortunately, she forgot about me. When it began to get dark outside, I climbed out the window and down the fire escape. I can't remember exactly what I did to deserve the punishment, but I was never put in the 'blue room' again!"

Despite Dike's occasional mischief, Philip Seely said he was a gentleman. "The only time I remember Dike deviating from that character was when he would fight with Joe Roddy. Dike heard that Joe, who was probably one of the toughest kids at Central School, was picking on smaller boys. Dike never could tolerate a bully. He told Joe if he wanted to pick on somebody, he should pick on somebody his own size. Dike and Joe would meet in the alley after school and go at it."

Dike's grade school teachers—all women, all single and all business—showed him increasing attention as his athletic proficiency was revealed. Dike credits his ability to distinguish right from wrong to the dedicated educators in the Centralia school district. He remembers every teacher he had from first through eighth grades. They were first grade—Miss Hanks; second grade—Miss McFarland; third grade—Miss Walters; fourth grade—Miss Edwards; fifth grade—Miss Chase; sixth grade—Miss Anderick; seventh grade—Miss Taake; and eighth grade—Miss Quilman and Miss Hazel. Lifelong friend and fellow teammate Bill Davies said the grade school principal, Mrs. Martha Watson, helped Dike dig a high-jump pit in a corner of the school yard. She would coach him during his free time on the playground.

Dike enjoyed recess even more than his peers when it became apparent he had a talent for high-jumping. In fifth grade, he high-jumped 4 feet, 9 inches. His obsession paid big dividends when, as a seventh-grader, he was offered a scholarship to Washington and Lee University in Lexington, Virginia. Newspapers throughout the country ran a story and photograph after Dike, at age 14, jumped 5-8¾ in his bare feet—while wearing street clothes. In eighth grade, Dike was high-jumping 5-11 and competing with the best jumper in the high school.

Even though it appeared he was a "natural," hours of practice and undaunted determination were what set him apart from the others. At an early age, Dike realized the necessity for self-discipline and established self-imposed training rules. "I can remember when I was 10 years old, even in the freezing weather, we'd go out and shoot baskets until dark. Once I remember sweeping the snow off the frozen ground so we could go on practicing."

The tall, lanky boy soon discovered his favorite time at school was spent on the playground or in the gym. While attending Central Grade School, in the heat of a rousing basketball game, Eddleman was given the nickname "Dike." One of his younger teammates shouted, "Dike! Pass it to Dike!" When pronounced with the true Centralia "Southern drawl," Dwight sounds very much like Dike.

When Eddleman was in seventh grade, Centralia High School basketball coach Arthur L. Trout saw him playing and told Dike he was good enough to be on his high school team. Dike said he was "walking on air for days." It was quite an accomplishment for a grade school player to receive that kind of compliment from one of the most highly regarded high school basketball coaches in Illinois history. Yet, Trout must have been aware of the young rookie as we read documentation of Eddleman's early talent written by Jim Thorp, sports editor of the *Centralia Sentinel* in the 1940s:

> By the time Eddleman was in the fourth grade he qualified for a berth on Centralia's lightweight basketball team (for boys weighing less than 100 pounds). In the fifth grade he played with the lightweight All-Stars from other city schools. When he was in the seventh grade, the All-Stars won seventeen and lost only one game. During a District tournament at Nashville, Illinois, Eddleman scored thirty-six points, a phenomenal number for a grade school player.

As early as fourth grade, Dike was an athletic curiosity. By age 10, he made the grade school basketball team and competed with boys in the seventh and eighth grades. As a high school freshman, he earned a starting position on the varsity basketball team. By his early teens, Eddleman was on his way to fame for his diverse athletic abilities. For a boy gifted with such talents, Centralia was certainly the right place to grow up.

Fortunately for Dike, Southern Illinois played a dominant role in Illinois basketball history during the 1930s and 1940s. If Centralia basketball were a disease, it would be a raging epidemic. Centralia fans still apply for a season ticket lottery to attend the high school's home basketball games. Boys are given basketballs at birth with the hope they will one day make the varsity team.

Perhaps no team better represents high school basketball than Centralia, which started its program in 1906. In 1982, the Naismith Memorial Basketball Hall of Fame recognized Centralia High School's national record of 1,500 victories. Centralia, under Coach Trout, won basketball championships in 1918, 1922 and 1942. In those days, the state tournament was played in Huff Gymnasium at the University of Illinois in Champaign-Urbana. There were no class divisions, only one championship game for the *entire* state.

In that era, the state tournament was dominated by teams from downstate, particularly Southern Illinois. On January 9, 1982, Centralia became the first high school team in the nation to earn 1,500 wins. After the 1996-97 season, Centralia High School had increased its record to 1,802 wins. To acquire that many victories, a team has to average 20 victories in 90 seasons.

Dike said his desire for winning was acquired in grade school. His first basketball coach, Bob McCall, was also the manual arts teacher. "Centralia had many marvelous teams, but the seeds for these fine young teams were planted at the elementary level. Coach McCall had a great knowledge of the game. He was fair, consistent and knew how to instill self-confidence. There was never any mention of the concept of self-esteem in those days. But the concept was alive and well at Central Grade School as Coach McCall molded his young players by setting a fine example for them."

Although Coach Arthur Trout received most of the glory for Centralia's winning basketball tradition, Coach Bob McCall should be credited, too. Most high school coaches benefit from strong grade school programs. Coach McCall provided such a "feeder" program for Coach Trout. There were seven grade schools in Centralia. Coach McCall played intercity games and interscholastic games between such towns as Greenville, Central City, Sandoval, Mount Vernon, New Baden and Christopher. In fourth grade, Dike played for Coach McCall during regular season games as well as on his all-star teams. These all-star teams were made up of the best players from the city's seven grade schools.

Dike said the grade schools emphasized winning. "Ethics were highly stressed, but the nature of the game taught us that winning was fun! I remember how our coaches and principals would challenge each other. One year, Mr. Purdue, Central School's principal, accepted a challenge between our grade school basketball team and Greenville's grade school team. Although time has erased the name of the Greenville principal from memory, I distinctly remember the game. The host principal, certain his cagers would win, bought a huge trophy for the first-place winners. Centralia won the contest and, believe it or not, the Greenville principal refused to give us the trophy!"

During these formative years, Dike and his friends admired the Centralia Demons, who played in an independent league. "We'd love to go to a place called Turner Hall and watch these black players. We looked up to these older guys. It was great entertainment because not only would these guys play basketball, but they would put on a show at halftime playing instruments and singing. Nights spent at Turner Hall would also provide a workout for us. By the time the games were over, it would be dark as pitch outside, and we'd all run home as fast as we could."

Bob Roddy and Bill Davies recalled an incident that demonstrated Dike's desire to be like the older boys. During Dike's eighth-grade summer, a bunch of high school boys decided to shave their heads. They were told if they shaved their heads and wore silk stockings on them, their hair would grow back curly. In Dike's case, it worked! If you take a close look at him, he still has wavy hair.

Bill Davies, who was appointed head basketball coach for the Centralia Orphans in 1959, was only the third basketball coach at Centralia High School since World War I. As a boy, he helped Eddleman with his *St. Louis Post-Dispatch* Sunday paper route. "We had a wooden cart with metal wheels that we would pull down the street, yelling 'Sunday paper!' at the top of our lungs trying to arouse as many people as we could. The papers sold for 10 cents apiece, and we got a penny per paper for selling them. We'd walk the length of town and try to hit Saint Mary's Catholic Church just as services ended. We sold a lot of papers out of that little wagon."

During those post-Depression years, money was scarce. The hourly wage in 1940 was only $1.40. Admission to the local movie theater was 10 cents; and for about $1.70, you could buy a new pair of denim overalls from Sears. Each penny earned selling papers added up. As Eddleman's athletic career soared, so did his paper route profits because people wanted to buy the *Dispatch* from the young athlete who was becoming the talk of the town. However, his profits never accumulated to the amount necessary for the new bicycle he coveted.

As a youth, Dike developed a craving for chocolate that partially was satisfied through his good friend, Bill Salisbury, whose aunt worked for a candy distributor. "I remember that Bill's aunt worked in a candy warehouse. She would get to keep packages of candy that would break open. Bill would always share his candy with me. During those years, even having a few pennies for candy was a luxury. It may have been through Bill that I acquired a sweet tooth. I remember eating more than my share of Heavyweight Champ candy bars. In high school, I used to go to H. B. "Shorty" Blanchard's hangout and buy a Heavyweight Champ candy bar and a quart of milk. That would be my lunch."

In 1938, Eddleman's father married a young woman named Jessie Wilson. Dike, his sister and his two half-sisters acquired a stepbrother, Stanley, and a stepsister, Diane, through the exchange of vows between Tom Eddleman and his bride from Tennessee. Since there were now six children in the household, Dike found himself wearing hand-me-downs from his stepbrother. His stepmother was a disciplinarian who often showed favoritism toward Stanley and Diane. She was a good cook who prided herself on simple but delicious fare.

The Depression was difficult, but Dike enjoyed life's simple pleasures. "I can remember coming home from school to a house filled with the scent of freshly baked pies or cinnamon rolls. During the summer months, we always had an abundance of fresh fruits and vegetables from my Dad's garden. My father loved to make homemade beer. I remember one hot summer night we heard explosions in our basement. We all ran downstairs to find that the bottles of his homemade brew had burst, and there were huge foamy splotches running down the basement walls. My father was a good man who enjoyed the simple pleasures in life.

I've been known to enjoy a cigar or two in my day. I acquired this habit from my Dad, who loved to light up a King Edward after dinner and sit in our back yard under this huge maple tree. I remember, as if it were yesterday, gathering around the radio and listening to 'The Shadow.' Life was very good in those days, and I feel extremely fortunate to have grown up in Centralia."

As a youngster, Dike was crazy about cowboy music. Among his idols were Tom Mix, Hoot Gibson, Hopalong Cassidy, Roy Rogers, Ken Maynard and Gene Autry. Dike often would croon a tune or at least attempt it. "Flip" Seely recalled a program presented at a banquet in honor of their graduation from Central Grade School. "When we graduated from grade school, our class was treated to a banquet at the Presbyterian Church at the corner of Broadway and Hickory in Centralia. We were all dressed in our Sunday best, and it was the first time I had worn a suit. We were treated to entertainment by a vocal quartet, comprised of Dike, Farrell Robinson, David Kinsell and Russell Ditterline. Dike, for as long as I can remember, liked what I believe was then called cowboy music. At any rate, they sang 'Gold Mine in the Sky,' which I believe was made popular by Gene Autry. Well, those guys sang like I played basketball—maybe worse. It was quite a memorable performance!"

In the summer of 1938, after Dike's eighth-grade year, life on Maple Street changed. After Tom Eddleman retired from the Illinois Central Railroad, he purchased 100 acres from a brother and moved the Eddleman clan back to the family farm in Dongola. Dike remained in Centralia under the guardianship of his half-sister, LaVonne Lichtenfeld, and her husband, John, so he could develop his athletic talents. The decision, encouraged by Coach Arthur Trout and Judge Fred Wham, proved to be a wise one.

Since LaVonne and her husband lived in a small apartment, Dike was invited to reside with a friend, Glenn "Opp" Thomas, for his first two years of high school. Glenn lived with his grandparents, who gladly took Dike in and treated him like one of the family. Mr. Thomas was a successful contractor who owned a rambling country home. Although Glenn was not athletic, he and Dike became good friends. Dike earned spending money doing odd jobs for his half-sisters, Dorothy and LaVonne. It wasn't until his junior year in high school that Dike moved in with LaVonne and John. That year, the Lichtenfelds moved from their apartment on North Locust into a house on the west side of town.

Dike was grateful to his half-sister and brother-in-law for allowing him to move in. He had his own room, which stayed cleaner than most because he was usually at school practicing or participating in a sport. Dike's room contained a desk, a chair, a dresser and a four-poster bed. On his dresser sat several pictures with inscriptions from some of Centralia's loveliest young ladies. In winter, his bedroom was the coldest room in the house because he liked to sleep without heat. Coach Trout told him he would stay healthier if he did that. The rest of the Lichtenfeld's residence was furnished with a beautiful collection of antiques. Dike was apprehensive about sitting in the more delicate furnishings because he was afraid he would break them. Although he had all the necessities during his high school years, Dike was living in a house, not a home.

Separation from his parents at age 15 was not an easy choice. However, the prospects of attending a one-room schoolhouse in Dongola, which would have eliminated any hope of athletic competition, made the decision more palatable. It was a culture shock for Dike to leave a family setting, to be placed with relative strangers and then to live with a couple who had no children. LaVonne's husband, John, encouraged Dike's athletic pursuits, having had an athletic background himself. Lichtenfeld played for Arthur Trout's 1922 Centralia state championship basketball team. The couple was happy to take in the young boy who showed so much athletic promise. However, Dike usually was left to fend for himself. Dinner was not always waiting for him when he came home, and he never had a mother who tucked him in at night.

Although Dike does not remember his mother, he inherited many of her characteristics. In a diary kept by one of his mother's relatives, there is a beautiful passage written after the death of Dike's mother, Alma, in March 1925. It reads, "She was of a kind and lovable disposition. She made friends wherever she went. None were too humble or lowly for her to greet with a smile. Her thoughts were ever for the happiness and comfort of others regardless of the sacrifices she had to make to do it. She was a faithful and devoted wife as well as a kind and loving mother. Although she had been in suffering and pain the greater part of the past five months, the last five weeks of which she was in unbearable agony, she bore it uncomplainingly and without murmuring until at last nature could sustain her no longer and she closed her tired eyes and gently fell asleep."

It is believed there are two elements that shape our character: nature and nurture. From the eulogy in the diary, it seems Dike is much like Alma: kind, loving, devoted and brave. The nurturing aspect of his childhood, on the other hand, created a need to feel loved. Dike discovered this need could be satisfied by the attention and admiration shown to him by his fans.

At this point in his life, Eddleman learned an indelible lesson: with the roses come the thorns. For a chance to compete and grasp the "golden ring," he had to leave his family at a tender and vulnerable stage in his life. Dike sacrificed growing up with his family for a chance at success. Athletics filled the void in his life caused by the inevitable loneliness and insecurity he experienced during his adolescence. It was a risk well taken as, in the next several years, he would develop into one of Illinois' finest prep stars. With the decision made to reside in Centralia, Dike was afforded the opportunity to attend Centralia High School and play for one of Illinois' most renowned high school coaches, Arthur L. Trout.

CHAPTER 2

THE INFLUENCE OF COACH TROUT

Dike Eddleman's most significant high school memory does not come from any single athletic event but, instead, from a friendship that influenced a lifetime of successful athletic and academic endeavors. Coach Arthur Lloyd Trout became a father figure, role model, mentor and friend to this young athlete. Dike provided the ability and the brawn; Trout supplied the experience and the wisdom. When their expertise was combined, it created a chemistry that ignited the enthusiasm of sports fans statewide. Looking at Coach Trout's roots gives definition to his coaching genius and enables one to draw distinct parallels between these sports legends.

Dike said Trout was a man of high ideals. "He wanted us to learn the value of team unity and the importance of playing together. That is the way he coached. The boys and the team came first, because he was a builder of men. Mr. Trout reminded us many times that his coaching philosophy was simple. He would claim, 'I just get you boys together, and we work with each other,'" Eddleman said.

When it came to coaching, Trout, who held a master's degree in education, was a self-proclaimed empiricist. He claimed he had no rigid coaching style. He followed the "rule of thumb" method, training his boys according to their abilities. He always stressed fundamentals, and he tried to guard against giving his players "mental indigestion." His general philosophy of life was idealistic: He believed that right was right in all circumstances.

Coach Trout believed athletic achievement and academic excellence were synonymous. He took pride in the number of his players who continued their educations past high school. Eddleman said Coach Trout emphasized equal time in the study hall and in the gym.

The son of a Christian minister and Latin teacher from Bruceville, Indiana, Trout acquired a lifelong love of reading from his father, who had an extensive library in their home. As a boy, Trout memorized lines of poetry and biblical Scriptures to sharpen his mental acuity. Eddleman was fascinated by Trout's ability to quote verse after verse from the classics. One of Trout's favorite poems was "If" by Rudyard Kipling, which he recited at the beginning of each season.

"IF"

If you can keep your head when all about you
Are losing theirs and blaming it on you,
If you can trust yourself when all men doubt you,
But make allowance for their doubting too;
If you can wait and not be tired by waiting,
Or being lied about, don't deal in lies,
Or being hated don't give way to hating,
And yet don't look too good, nor talk too wise:

If you can dream—and not make dreams your master;
If you can think—and not make thoughts your aim,
If you can meet with Triumph and Disaster
And treat those two impostors just the same;

If you can bear to hear the truth you've spoken
Twisted by knaves to make a trap for fools,
Or watch the things you gave your life to, broken,
And stoop and build 'em up with worn-out tools:

If you can make one heap of all your winnings;
And risk it on one turn of pitch-and-toss,
And lose, and start again at your beginnings
And never breathe a word about your loss;
If you can force your heart and nerve and sinew
To serve your turn long after they are gone,
And so hold on when there is nothing in you
Except the Will which says to them: "Hold on!"

If you can talk with crowds and keep your virtue,
Or walk with Kings—nor lose the common touch,
If neither foes nor loving friends can hurt you,
If all men count with you, but none too much;
If you can fill the unforgiving minute
With sixty seconds' worth of distance run,
Yours is the Earth and everything that's in it,
And—which is more—you'll be a Man, my son!

(Kipling, *The Home Book of Verse,* 1912).

Ironically, this poem, which Eddleman can quote verbatim, became his creed. "If" made a lasting impression on Dike's life because it taught him that how a person lives may be as important as what he achieves.

Although Eddleman and Trout had different reasons for participating in sports, both turned to athletics early. Trout's childhood was not easy because, within a year, he caught typhoid fever and diphtheria. After suffering these childhood diseases, he turned to athletics to strengthen his frail body. Trout was a senior at Bruceville High School in 1905 when basketball, created by Dr. James A. Naismith, swept through Indiana like a prairie fire. Trout once told Dike about the first basketball game he saw. It was played at night on an outdoor court illuminated by oil lanterns hanging from trees. Trout said he immediately fell in love with the sport.

After Trout graduated from high school in 1909, he became a teacher to earn money so he could enroll at Indiana University. There, he planned to delve into some of the new physical education courses. Trout was a gym rat. He took courses in wrestling, tumbling and any other form of athletics being offered. He also participated in football, baseball and track.

After finishing college, Trout looked for a job. Doctors promoted the theory that it was dangerous for athletes to suddenly give up their strenuous lifestyle for one of relaxation. Trout was a believer! He took a teaching job at Centralia High School, which had an enrollment of only 200 students, because the school wanted a coach as well as a teacher. Trout thought an active coaching career would help keep him in shape.

Before graduating from college in 1914, Trout spent much of his free time with Bloomington native Freda Sears, a talented young woman who played the piano beautifully. Trout promised his fiancee he soon would return for her. Being a man of his word, Trout returned around Christmastime to Bloomington and married Sears on Christmas Eve.

The Trouts returned to Illinois and lived in a small apartment. Later, he and his wife bought a home only one block from the school. Trout escaped from the pressures of a highly stressful career by surrounding himself with his family, his books and his dogs. He was a private man, and Trout's desire for privacy led to many rumors and myths that circulated around school and the town. Don Schnake, author of a biography titled *Trout: The Old Man and the Orphans,* wrote, "Whispers that the Trouts had never liked Centralia still float about. Some said that they never unpacked their good china and silver because they always planned to move the following year."

The Trouts had three daughters, Virginia, Dorothy and Pat, and a son, Robert, who died at birth. In his biography, Trout's youngest daughter, Pat, described her father as "a devoted husband and a kind and loving father who showed us great tenderness." Trout was a gentleman and a gentle man. His daughters recalled sitting in the back seat of their car while their father delivered baskets of food to a widow and her children. He not only spoke about the "golden rule," he lived it. With his own money, he ordered coal for a needy family. He also bought eyeglasses and dentures for others.

Following Trout's example, Dike also has been recognized for his sensitivity and compassion. Perhaps this letter received from Wayne Barham, a college classmate and friend, best illustrates Eddleman's concern and empathy for others.

January 19, 1993

Hi!

I am the nephew of Juanita Hangaard. Her husband was Harold (Swede) Hangaard. My Marine outfit made landings on Bougainville, Guam, and Iwo in World War II. A hand grenade blinded me and I got sight back in one eye. I came back to the University of Illinois and was a P.E. major. Perhaps you don't remember this, but I always will be grateful for what you did for me at that time. My depth perception was terrible as I learned to adjust with one eye. One class gave me problems, because we were graded on winning or losing games in Indoor Recreational Sports. Of course, with your reflexes, you could beat anyone at anything. But in handball, where we were alone, you let me beat you—to help my grade. I can't remember the teacher, but I'm sure we weren't fooling him—but he marked you down with the losses and gave me the wins. I'll never forget that.

I later coached football and basketball in high schools at
Robinson, Illinois, Springfield, South Dakota, Rhinelander, Wisconsin, and also at Buena Vista College in Iowa. I transferred
from the University of Illinois after three years and was the
kicker and punter for the University of South Dakota (Springfield) football team in 1949. The last twenty years, I was head
of the Social and Behavioral Sciences Department at USD/S. I
tell you all this to let you know that I feel you were a great
influence on me. I have always admired your leadership, athletic ability, and modesty . . .

Sincerely,
Wayne Barham

There have been other magnanimous deeds by Eddleman
such as the time he missed in the high jump during a college
meet so Jim Corwin, a courageous young athlete who lost an arm
in a hunting accident, could win. By winning that event, Corwin
became eligible to letter in track.

Dike's wife, Teddy, said her husband often was asked to visit
young patients at local hospitals. "There was never any hesita-
tion on Dike's part. He would gladly go with gifts in hand and a
smile that would brighten anyone's day. I particularly remember
one youngster who was suffering from severe burns. Dike took
the boy an autographed ball and encouraged him to be 'tough'.
A telephone call from the parents weeks later praised Dike for
his kindness. The mother told Dike she would always be grateful
to him for lifting her son's spirits at a very critical time."

Because Trout was an eloquent speaker, he was invited to
banquets around the state. His ability to speak extemporane-
ously was a finely developed art. He told wonderful stories, and
his audiences were enthralled. It made no difference to whom
or where he spoke, he always wore his coaching attire, which
consisted of a well-worn suit, white shirt, necktie, black high-top
shoes and a battered felt hat.

After his athletic success, Eddleman, too, became a popular speaker, traveling to banquets and meetings statewide. By his own admission, Eddleman does not describe his speechmaking as eloquent. Dr. George Ross remembers traveling the banquet circuit with Dike during his senior year in college. "It was great fun going to speaking engagements with him. He had an old Ford convertible that we drove to these affairs. The meals were fantastic, so I hardly ever turned down an invitation to go along. Halfway to our destination, I'd nonchalantly ask Dike what he planned to say in his speech. His reply was invariably, 'I'll just think of it as I go along.' Audiences were so eager to hear him speak, they never seemed to care if it was rehearsed or not. They would always be satisfied because the message came straight from the heart."

Coach Trout wasn't a social climber; neither is Dike. When it came to social status, both Trout and Eddleman remained unpretentious despite the glory and the limelight that victory often brings. They both believed in accepting people for what they are instead of who they are.

Coach Trout had definite ideas about his players' social lives. He told his players they might go stale without any social life. But he insisted their health and well-being should be their top priority—much to the chagrin of the female students attending Centralia High School. "I never learned how to dance," Dike said. "I think Coach Trout was happy about that. He would tell us there was nothing wrong with dancing, but too much socializing could lead to unacceptable behavior such as smoking and drinking."

No matter what kind of player you were, if Coach Trout caught you breaking his rules, you were off the team. Dike said, "I remember the closest I ever came to doing something wrong was when I chewed Beech-Nut tobacco. One road game, I took a coffee can (to spit in) on the bus. As Coach walked down the aisle of the bus, he kicked over my can of spit. I held my breath—afraid he would bench me. I nearly swallowed my chew!" Trout never said anything about that incident, but he had removed boys from the team for smoking cigarettes.

"Trout treated his players like sons," Dike said. "Trout tried to keep us healthy. When we did get sick, he tried to cure us. I remember having a terrible chest cold during one basketball season. Trout took me across the street to Amos Whitlock's grocery store one morning after practice when I couldn't stop coughing. He asked for a big slice of pork rind, which he generously covered with dry mustard and camphor. He then pinned it to my underwear and told me to leave it on all day. The crazy thing is, it cured my cold! Coach Trout had lots of advice on keeping us in topnotch condition. He noticed that many of us had extremely dry skin from taking so many showers. One morning, he brought in two gallons of olive oil and told us to rub some on our bodies after showering. It cured our dry skin, but we had to be careful not to sit too close to the radiators during classes because if we got too hot we really started smelling ripe!"

As dean of boys, football coach, basketball coach, athletic director and master teacher, Trout ruled supreme from 1914-51 at Centralia High School. Trout's social studies and civics classes were overflowing as his reputation on and off the playing field became known. He taught classes with the same finesse with which he coached. Don Schnake, a former player for Coach Trout, said, "Arthur Trout personified the positive aspects of athletics within the education experience; moreover, he did it with color, drama and a vivid imagination. Players and students alike respected him for his integrity, knowledge, discipline and consistency."

Likewise, Eddleman was respected for possessing many of those virtues. Dr. William Lindenburg, a Centralia dentist, recalled the summer of 1946. "Dike used to practice punting footballs at the high school field where we almost always had a morning neighborhood baseball game. If Dike was punting, we would go to the opposite end of the field and shag the footballs in a large canvas bag and take them back to him to kick again. When he became tired, he would come down to the southeast end of the field where our dirt-base diamond was and pitch baseballs to us. All of us younger boys idolized Dike, and in his white shorts, football shoes and with sweat glistening on his bare arms and chest in the sun, he was the closest thing to a Greek God we had ever seen! He knew how to be friendly, modest, humble and yet was able to command respect for his many achievements."

Trophies, medals and honors were common booty for Trout and Eddleman. Trout's coaching expertise helped him fill several trophy cases at Centralia High School. His 37-year tenure as basketball coach at Centralia produced 809 victories, 10 state tournament teams and three state championships. His teams won 25 games at least 15 times, and they claimed more than 65 championship trophies. Trout's record remains impressive even by modern standards.

ARTHUR TROUT'S BASKETBALL RECORD DURING HIS TENURE AT CENTRALIA HIGH SCHOOL

YEAR	W - L	YEAR	W - L
1915	16 - 12	1934	30 - 5
1916	18 - 5	1935	14 - 19
1917	24 - 4	1936	18 - 14
1918	23 - 4*	1937	26 - 4
1919	17 - 3	1938	17 - 13
1920	30 - 3	1939	29 - 14
1921	26 - 5	1940	29 - 5
1922	26 - 4*	1941	44 - 2
1923	9 - 17	1942	34 - 6*
1924	26 - 7	1943	26 - 6
1925	28 - 7	1944	6 - 24

1926	16 - 15	1945	24 - 13
1927	21 - 5	1946	30 - 10
1928	18 - 14	1947	32 - 7
1929	23 - 3	1948	19 - 9
1930	12 - 17	1949	15 - 12
1931	15 - 10	1950	21 - 7
1932	11 - 17	1951	9 - 4
1933	28 - 4		

*State champions

Trout's record confirms his passion for basketball. After the Eddleman Era, the Illinois High School Association decreed a limit on the number of games a high school is allowed to play each season.

Trout received official recognition for his athletic accomplishments by being selected as a member of the following halls of fame: Centralia Sports Hall of Fame, Illinois Football Coaches Hall of Fame, Illinois Basketball Hall of Fame, *Evansville (Indiana) Courier and Press* Tri-State Hall of Fame and the National High School Sports Hall of Fame. Following in his mentor's footsteps, Eddleman received similar recognition.

Obviously, Trout was doing something right. Although his coaching methods sometimes were unorthodox, he always walked away a winner. Pat Harmon, former sports editor of the *Cincinnati Post* and historian for the National Football Foundation's College Football Hall of Fame said: "The most remarkable person I met on the high school basketball circuit was Coach Arthur L. Trout, who won state championships in 1918, 1922 and 1942. His football teams had bizarre plays, one of which ended with the center carrying the ball after a lateral pass from the quarterback. His basketball teams used a full-court press on defense and a shoot-and-rebound attack on offense. His players used a two-handed push shot which was executed with their feet and knees together, the body centrally balanced, and the ball held against the face just below eye level."

The two-handed push shot became better known as the "Kiss Shot." Eddleman and Trout's "Kiss Shot" became a notorious combination as the prep star scored with deadly accuracy. The name was appropriate because it appeared the players kissed the ball as they arched it nearly to the rafters. "What's funny," said Eddleman, "is that after a game our chins and the tips of our noses would be black with dirt. We shot often during games because Coach Trout told us to shoot anytime we were open and past the center line."

"Trout had figured it out scientifically, or at least that's what he told us. The idea of the 'Kiss Shot' was to shoot the ball with a high arch. The theory, as Trout explained it, was that two things might happen when it came down. Both were beneficial to the offense. First, the ball had a better chance of going through the hoop because its nearly vertical descent made a bigger target out of the hoop; second, if it hit the rim, it would bounce straight back up into the air allowing us to get a running approach to the backboard, thereby executing a higher vertical jump on the rebound." Whether Trout's hypothesis was valid, the technique certainly worked for Dike and his teammates.

Today's high school players shoot three-pointers from beyond a 19-foot line. Dike said, "I'd have loved that in my day! I don't remember shooting many from closer than that."

During Trout's reign, he never changed his method of coaching. When asked by reporters about his tenure, he confided: "God was good to me. Anytime I'd have a few bad years and would be wondering if the school board was going to fire me, the Lord would send me a Lowell Spurgeon or a Dike Eddleman, and I'd be saved."

Trout was a master of psychology and wit. His showmanship bordered on theatrics. When the "Downtown Coaches Association," as he referred to the armchair quarterbacks of Centralia, thought a freshman was not seasoned enough to play varsity, Trout would take the boy to center court wearing a garland of carrots and other vegetables and sprinkle it with salt. Trout then declared the player was "seasoned" and could play. Such an event took place in 1944 with Orphan basketball player Charles "Pig" Oland. Trout knew the fans wanted to be entertained, and he never failed to provide a great show.

At the height of Eddleman's high school success, opponents targeted him for malicious physical and mental assaults. These attacks disturbed Coach Trout. Before a big game with rival Mount Vernon, Trout entered the dressing room carrying a miniature saddle that he tied on Eddleman's back before the team took the floor. During warm-ups, Coach Trout gathered the referees and opposing coaches. He said, "Gentlemen, each game I see different forms of rough tactics used against my boy Dike. Let's be open about this. If you want to ride him, ride him now while he's wearing a saddle. When the game begins and the saddle comes off, I want the riding to stop. Let's just play basketball!" His point well made, the game generally proceeded without incident.

Orphan teammate Bill Davies vividly recalled one contest at Marion, Illinois, in which Eddleman had to be protected from a spectator. "This incident happened between Dike and a friend of mine from Marion named Diz Carlton. The gym was packed, as usual, and the game was a close one. When the officials weren't looking, Diz hit Dike with an elbow to the stomach. It had to have hurt, but, as usual, Dike didn't complain. On the next out-of-bounds play, Diz was guarding Dike. As Dike heaved the ball inbounds, everybody's eyes followed the ball down the court, and Dike popped Diz in the mouth. With that, Diz Carlton's mother came rushing out of the stands trying to hit Dike over the head with her umbrella." As usual, Trout conferred with the referees and order quickly was restored.

Trout, who maintained the highest code of sportsmanship, taught his players that self-defense was one thing; blatant misconduct during a game was another matter. "Unsportsmanlike behavior was not tolerated by Trout," Dike said. "During a basketball game we played in East Peoria, Corwin Clatt, a strong kid who later played football for the University of North Dakota, ripped my shirt and took more than his share of cheap shots. We had been invited to stay for sandwiches after the game, but Trout refused to stay because he thought East Peoria's lack of sportsmanship was appalling. He blamed the referees for letting things get out of hand. When he found out that they had burned a dummy wearing a jersey with my number on it in effigy the night before, Trout was furious that we had even shown up to play the game. Despite a victory, that was a dismal night. On the way home from East Peoria, we got lost, and our bus ended up in East St. Louis."

Not only clever on the court, Trout knew what the public wanted to hear and never passed up a chance to speak with reporters. When asked why the Centralia Cardinals became the Centralia Orphans, Trout told one reporter the name came from a Chicago sports writer who described the Centralia team while it was playing in 1942 at the Pontiac tournament. He claimed that they looked like orphans in their bedraggled uniforms, tired and dirty from a long trip, "but they sure could play basketball!" On another occasion, Trout said the name came to him in the early 1920s when he saw Lillian Gish star in the movie *Orphans of the Storm*. Yet another *Centralia Sentinel* article reported the nickname came from an earlier time in Centralia High School athletics when the school's administration was not supportive of the sports program. The apathy shown to the athletes by the administration and the school board caused Coach Trout to remark the school practically had disowned the boys, and they had become like "orphans," a colorful name that remains even after several changes of the administrative guard.

This cleverest of coaches affectionately was referred to as "Mister Trout" by his players, "the Old Man" by his fans, and "King

Arthur" by the media. It was only fitting that a monument be built in his honor. In 1938, when Centralia discovered it was sitting on top of a huge oil field, this wish became a reality. By 1940, nearly 2,000 wells pumped away in farm fields, back yards and vacant lots as the Lake Centralia field, then producing 300,000 barrels a day, grew into the nation's largest oil field.

With this prosperity came a new facility designed to house the high school basketball team. Appropriately it was christened Trout Gymnasium. Above the gym's entrance is a huge stained-glass window displaying figures of two basketball players. In the design appear the Latin words, "Mens Sana In Corpore Sano In Omnia Paratur," which proclaim the school's philosophy: "A sound mind in a sound body prepares one for all things in life." This facility serves as a legacy to a coach who was worshiped by his adoring fans and players in a community where basketball is deemed a religious experience. Trout and a bevy of basketball teams provided many thrilling nights of roundball madness in that gymnasium. It was in "Trout's House" that Centralia's basketball tradition was nurtured.

Trout's reputation, perhaps, remains his finest tribute. At the re-dedication of Trout Gymnasium on Sunday, October 16, 1994, featured speaker Lowell Spurgeon reminded a pensive audience, "It is impressive that Arthur Trout still has a profound influence upon many of us today." Mr. Spurgeon read a letter he recently had received from his grandson, stating how lucky Lowell had been to have had Trout as a mentor. His grandson continued to write, "I realize how lucky I am to have you as my grandfather. *You* are my Coach Trout." For the Lowell Spurgeon family, Trout's influence has spanned four generations.

Author Don Schnake paid homage to his former coach and hero by writing a special poem that he read at the re-dedication program. His work is titled, "Ode to the House of Trout."

My father changed my life one night
In the year of '38,
When he took this wide-eyed ten year old
Through the ticket gate

Of this grand and noble building,
A landmark from the start.
It's always been the focal point—
Centralia's very heart.

It drips with rich tradition
This place of many thrills,
With mem'ries for a million fans ...
The cheers, the tears, the chills.
Folks turned out to root and shout
At things they'd ne'er forget ...
Like kiss shots through the rafters
When they'd rocket through the net.

Like the band when it whipped up spirit
With those marches blazing loud.
When waves of sheer excitement
Electrified the crowd.

Little boys had heroes then
They could see and touch and hear.
I found mine to idolize—
Those greats of yesteryear.

Raised on the likes of the Wonder Five
And the Champions of '42
As a red-blooded lad, I simply had
To try and do it, too.

The world of sports has been my life
Since that night I became a fan,
And I owe it all to basketball
And this gym where it all began.

Each person who grew up down here,
Since they built this stately place,
Has a ton of reminiscences
That time just won't erase.

Oh, the sounds these walls have heard
And the pageantry they've seen—
As youngsters learned the game of life
By playing hard and clean.

We've come to praise a legend:
This building bears his name;
He's grinning down from high above—
From Heaven's Hall of Fame.
If we measure a man by the lives he's shaped
Instead of the games he's won,
Mister Trout would still stand out—
Would still be Number One.
It's only fit and proper
That we dedicate this gym,
So that future generations
Will all remember him.

So they'll ne'er forget this special man
With his fatherly approach . . .
This truly gifted teacher . . .
This celebrated coach.

Endless streams of people
Have built Centralia's lore,
But three names rise above the rest
And will forevermore.

We're proud to share this moment
With the best beyond a doubt;
Lowell Spurgeon, Dike Eddleman,
And the spirit of Arthur Trout.

Praise be for this occasion
That keeps the torch aglow.
It reminds us of our heritage
That started long ago.

I charge you keepers of the flame
To never let it die.
Glory in your storied past—
Those precious days gone by.

And Hail once more to the Cardinal—
Centralia's battle cry—
May your pride and spirit always soar
Like eagles in the sky.

> —Don Schnake
> Centralia High School
> Class of 1946

Dike attended the re-dedication. As a bright autumn sun filtered through the windows that October Sunday, the cardinal pillars of Trout Gym took on a brighter hue. The spirit of Arthur Trout *was* smiling that day along with his daughter, Pat, many friends and former athletes who had gathered to honor him.

Coach Trout would be pleased to know that alongside the many trophies that adorn the halls of Trout Gymnasium stands a shrine to one of his finest players. In a glass case, next to a portrait of Coach Trout, hangs the retired jersey of Centralia's famous No. 40, Thomas Dwight "Dike" Eddleman.

Coach and athlete. Mentor and prodigy. They were alike in so many ways: talented, clever, compassionate, idealistic, disciplined and godly. Trout and Eddleman. They were two kindred spirits eager to compete and savor victory.

CHAPTER 3

THE ROAD TO
ATHLETIC EXCELLENCE

Under Coach Trout's guidance, Eddleman proceeded on the road to athletic excellence, developing
physically, academically and spiritually. After enrolling
at Centralia High School in 1938, expectations ran high
for the shy and unassuming freshman. Although his
high school career would be an accomplished one, it
was not without its trials and tribulations. As he played
the first football game of his freshman season, hearts
must have skipped beats and gasps for breath must have been
heard throughout the crowd when Eddleman was downed from
behind on a late hit. Eddleman, who had thrilled fans minutes
before by scoring the first two touchdowns against Johnston City,
was sidelined with a knee injury that kept him from playing high
school football until his senior year.

Training was an integral part of Trout's program. Before
games, Trout's athletes had their ankles painted with tincture of
benzoin. He then wrapped their ankles, like prized racehorses,
using roll after roll of athletic tape. Coach Trout said there was
no reason to wait until after the ankle was injured to care for it.
Tincture of benzoin, an inexpensive antiseptic that stained the
athletes' legs brown for days, probably served more as a badge of

courage than a medicinal aid. Trout used it generously, and Dike said "it burned like hell if the skin was broken." Unfortunately, neither tape nor antiseptic provided protection against a serious knee injury.

Trout's concern was evident after Eddleman's football mishap. Although Dike continued playing basketball and running track with a knee brace, the pain he suffered caused him and his coach great concern. Trout decided the two would travel to Ann Arbor, Michigan, the summer after Eddleman's sophomore year so knee surgery could be performed by Dr. John Hammond, one of the best orthopedic surgeons. Arrangements were made by Centralia's team physician, Dr. William Gamble, a University of Michigan alumnus. Financial support for the trip, the medical procedure and a six-week recuperation period was provided by Centralia High School and the local Lions Club.

"By today's standards, my knee surgery would seem very primitive," Dike said. "That kind of knee surgery was considered a major operation then, and I certainly wouldn't have had it performed had I not received help from Trout and the community. The operation itself lasted eight hours. The worst part of it was my reaction to the anesthetic when I woke up. It nearly killed me! In those days, they used ether to put a patient under. I remember that as I regained consciousness I was deathly ill from the side effects of the ether."

After his operation, Eddleman was not allowed to return to football until his senior year. Loren Tate, former sports editor of the *Champaign-Urbana News-Gazette*, recalled: "That senior year, after two years away from football, Eddleman sparked a 13-7 win with an 80-yard run, a 65-yard run and a drop kick for the extra point ... and he saved the game with an interception on the goal line." Joining the Orphan football team as a halfback and a punter, Eddleman finished his senior football season scoring 127 points. He also was named captain of the 1942 All-State football team. Not bad for a kid who got to play only one year of high school football. Obviously, Dike's knee surgery was successful, but his positive mental attitude and desire kept him in the game. Dike thrived on the thrill of competition and relished the attention and adulation of his fans. "The essential key to the Eddleman saga," said "Flip" Seely, "was his genuine character. By his senior year of high school, he had reached national prominence. Mind you, this was long before television and ESPN. Despite all the attention he received, he never forgot his friends. One excellent example of that occurred at a Centralia football game his senior year when Centralia played at Peoria. A friend and I were devout 'Eddlemaniacs,' so we hitchhiked all the way to Peoria to see the game. After Dike had played an excellent contest, my friend and I went over to congratulate him. He was dripping with sweat and exhausted, as you can imagine. When he found out we had hitchhiked to the game, he said, 'Wait here a minute.' He then sprinted half the length of the football field to ask another friend if he could give us a ride home. Running back across the field, he seemed as happy about finding us a ride home as he was about winning the game. I believe it is this sincere quality that impresses those who know Dike."

Despite Dike's knee injury, Herman Masin in *Varsity* magazine referred to him as a "four-alarm athletic fire and the greatest one-man gang since Superman." Although this "super kid" excelled in several sports, basketball was his favorite. As a high school freshman, Eddleman earned a starting position on varsity and proceeded to set a state record by scoring 24 points in a state basketball tournament game at Huff Gymnasium at the University of Illinois. In 1939, Bert Bertine, sports editor of the *Champaign-Urbana Courier,* wrote: "Perhaps the most amazing thing about Mr. Eddleman is that he is only a freshman. Rare it is when a freshman makes a varsity team, and then setting a state record to boot makes one wonder what this young man will do when he grows up! A good-looking lad, Eddleman, known as 'Baby Snooks' by his teammates, stands 6 feet even and weighs 160 pounds."

Eddleman said several factors influenced his high school sports career. First, there was Arthur Trout, who experienced his prime coaching years during the Eddleman Era. "Coach Trout was a motivator from the word go," Eddleman said. "He gave everyone a pair of 98-cent sneakers and a basketball at the beginning of the year. That was impressive to a guy like me who only got a new pair of overalls and a new pair of tennis shoes at Christmastime. He felt playing basketball would keep us in shape, no matter what other sports we wanted to play. He expected us to stay physically and mentally prepared year-round, especially at tournament time. During sectionals, he would set up cots in the gym, and the team would sleep there. With plenty of funds available, we would literally 'eat and sleep' basketball. Trout would feed the team, making sure we ate right. We could eat as much as we wanted, and I remember eating two or three T-bone steaks at a sitting."

Another factor that added to his high school success was a closeness brought about during World War II. The war united the home front. Centralia supported the war locally and nationally. Dike played when people were eager to find heroes. With war clouds looming everywhere, people searched for a ray of sunshine in an otherwise ominous world. Centralians found brief moments of hope and happiness at prep athletic events.

"Another factor that added to my success was my good fortune in playing with a group of extremely talented teammates. We were all friends because we'd been playing together since the fourth grade. Then, there was the construction of Trout Gymnasium. It was, and still is, a magnificent arena for basketball. I believe these factors, including a winning tradition, contributed to my success in high school."

Playing in the newly constructed gym boosted everyone's morale. Trout Gym was unique in its day. With a capacity for 2,800 fans, there are three rows of seats, complete with arm rests, on either side of the court. Even today, these seats serve as a status symbol for those desiring the best vantage point in the house. In the 1940s, high school basketball games were the best show in town. There were few alternatives, and Trout Gym was *the* place to be on game night. Adults dressed in their Sunday best because the games were considered a social event. Young and old alike stood in line hoping to be lucky enough to purchase a ticket to enter the friendly confines.

"Trout Gym had a character that stimulated a player's adrenaline," Eddleman said. "The seats and bleachers would always fill up first. Then the remaining fans would sit wherever they could find a space. There was a balcony that went all the way around the top of the gym. Students would sit with their legs dangling over the sides, getting a bird's-eye view of the action. I'm sure that at nearly every home game, Trout Gym would be packed with several hundred people over capacity. Fans would sit or stand anywhere just to see the game. Those who weren't lucky enough to get inside would have to listen to the game outside the gym as it was broadcast over the radio on loud-speakers. We had a spectacular band that added to the festive mood. I have always loved music! When that 60-member band played 'Hail to the Cardinal,' I felt like I could jump up and touch the rafters!"

During Dike's freshman year, he and four seniors played their first basketball game in Trout Gym. Setting a state basketball scoring record his first year was only a sample of what was to come. His sophomore basketball season was even more impressive. By his junior year, game results were reported in the local newspaper listing home scores first, followed by the visitor's scores and then Eddleman's individual point totals. At the end of the regular 1940-41 basketball season, box scores read as follows:

1940-41 CENTRALIA HIGH SCHOOL
BASKETBALL RECORD

Centralia	- 33	Ashley	- 16	Eddleman	- 11
Centralia	- 25	Taylorville	- 34	Eddleman	- 7
Centralia	- 52	Sandoval	- 19	Eddleman	- 15
Centralia	- 67	East Peoria	- 20	Eddleman	- 25
Centralia	- 71	Vandalia	- 26	Eddleman	- 26
Centralia	- 55	Springfield	- 26	Eddleman	- 28
Centralia	- 54	W. Frankfort	- 26	Eddleman	- 24
Centralia	- 61	Springfield	- 17	Eddleman	- 32
Centralia	- 42	Salem	- 17	Eddleman	- 17
Centralia	- 48	Beardstown	- 28	Eddleman	- 18
Centralia	- 52	Paris	- 30	Eddleman	- 18
Centralia	- 45	Taylorville	- 28	Eddleman	- 22
Centralia	- 46	Carbondale	- 19	Eddleman	- 25
Centralia	- 65	Aledo	- 24	Eddleman	- 18
Centralia	- 45	Clinton	- 30	Eddleman	- 20
Centralia	- 45	Peoria Manual	- 29	Eddleman	- 21
Centralia	- 41	Flora	- 20	Eddleman	- 15
Centralia	- 54	Herrin	- 19	Eddleman	- 23
Centralia	- 41	Mt. Vernon	- 23	Eddleman	- 21
Centralia	- 34	Carbondale	- 14	Eddleman	- 17
Centralia	- 44	Benton	- 31	Eddleman	- 28
Centralia	- 38	East Peoria	- 33	Eddleman	- 11
Centralia	- 59	Marion	- 18	Eddleman	- 26
Centralia	- 43	Harrisburg	- 17	Eddleman	- 25
Centralia	- 68	Ashley	- 14	Eddleman	- 23
Centralia	- 67	Urbana	- 27	Eddleman	- 23
Centralia	- 41	W. Frankfort	- 33	Eddleman	- 14
Centralia	- 60	Sandoval	- 6	Eddleman	- 26
Centralia	- 48	Mt. Vernon	- 24	Eddleman	- 19
Centralia	- 56	Herrin	- 30	Eddleman	- 18
Centralia	- 30	Harrisburg	- 29	Eddleman	- *
Centralia	- 60	Benton	- 27	Eddleman	- 25
Centralia	- 51	Marion	- 27	Eddleman	- 14
Centralia	- 68	Beardstown	- 25	Eddleman	- 30
Centralia	- 60	Salem	- 18	Eddleman	- 27
Centralia	- 100	Vandalia	- 36	Eddleman	- 42

Total - 1869   **Total** - 860   **Total** - 754

Averages - 51.91   23.88   21.54

                                                (35 games)

*None of first team played in this game.

His freshman year, the team's record was 17-13. His sophomore year, it was 29-14. During Dike's junior year, the Orphans won *42* games and lost only two! Perhaps because of pressure from the media and the overwhelming publicity Eddleman received, one of his most unforgettable high school basketball memories is not of a victory but of a defeat. During the 1940-41 basketball season, the Orphans were scheduled to play the host Taylorville Tornadoes. Bill Hopper, a Taylorville native and an Illinois alumnus, said Trout dropped a bombshell during the team's pregame instruction. Coach Trout said he planned to start Eddleman and four second-team members.

After the first quarter, the Orphans trailed by six points. During the second quarter, the usual starters played, and a second-team player took Eddleman's place. At halftime, Centralia trailed Taylorville by 14 points, a tremendous deficit in those days.

The Orphans returned to the locker room to await Coach Trout, but the coach never showed. Instead, he sat on the bench all alone. Halftime talks were crucial because coaches were not allowed to talk to the team during timeouts. With a great deal of enthusiasm, the Orphans vowed to show the old man by going out in the second half and winning the game.

At the start of the third quarter, Trout ordered the regular starters, minus Eddleman, into the game. By the end of the quarter, the Orphans trailed by 18 points. With about five minutes remaining, Coach Trout put the first team, including Eddleman, into the game.

After trailing by 22 points, Centralia ended up losing by nine. When the Orphans returned to their locker room, it was empty. There were no reporters, no fans. Another important Trout truism painfully was illustrated: Everybody loves a winner, and the Orphans would be winners only if they played together as a *team*.

Coach Trout eventually returned to the locker room. As much as he would have liked to have beaten Taylorville and Coach Dolph Stanley, Trout explained the moral of that evening's lesson.

Eddleman recalled Trout's simple speech: "Boys, I wanted you to learn one thing here tonight—that the first team needs Eddleman just as much as Eddleman needs the other four players."

That speech was made after the second game of Dike's junior season. The rationale for Trout's actions in Taylorville was explained by Jack Ryan, who wrote a sports column called "The Roundup." In it, he said, "From the Taylorville defeat, there emerged a sense of team play that never faltered. As the season got under way, Coach A. L. Trout faced the same problem that Fritz Crisler had with Tom Harmon, that Bob Zuppke had with Red Grange, that every coach is confronted with when a boy of consummate skill comes along. The one boy gets the plaudits, the other boys must be made content to don a cloak of anonymity." Trout was not about to let jealousy rear its ugly green head. A game was lost to Taylorville, but a basketball team was created.

In another 1941 basketball game, Centralia was scheduled to play the Harrisburg Bulldogs. Coach Trout decided to play only second-team members. The Orphans' success that season was due to their depth of talented players. On Friday, February 14, 1941, Coach Trout intentionally forgot the first-team players' uniforms. Because Centralia already had clinched the conference championship, he said the team had everything to lose by risking injury to a starter. However, a moral victory could be gained through a second-squad win. The Harrisburg gym, referred to as the "pit," had a low stage beneath the basket on one end, permanent bleachers at the other end and brick walls hemming in the remaining sides. It was a tremendous morale booster when the second team beat the Bulldogs 30-29 in a down-to-the-buzzer thriller. Once again, Coach Trout knew best.

About 3,000 fans attended an incredible scoring spectacle on Saturday, March 1, 1941, in Trout Gymnasium as Centralia routed rival Vandalia 100-36. Dike scored 42 points, boosting his season total to 751 and breaking a 10-year-old state record set by Bill Haarlow of Chicago.

As Eddleman scored his 30th point in that game, it wasn't necessary to announce he had tied Haarlow's record. Most fans kept track of Eddleman's point totals daily. The crowd went berserk when Eddleman sped down the court for the basket that eclipsed Haarlow's mark. From that moment, fans whooped and cheered like crazed maniacs! When Eddleman leaped high into the air to sink the shot that put Centralia's score at the century mark, the 3,000 fans let loose with the wildest roar that had ever echoed throughout Trout Gymnasium! That was the last regularly scheduled game for the 1941 "Wonder Five" team, and it was a fitting end. The "Wonder Five" and the talented reserves were the kind of team that most men only dream of coaching!

"Trout had worked his coaching genius building up our self-confidence, while at the same time keeping us levelheaded. There were many times that year that we could have blown our opponents away," Eddleman said. "But that definitely wasn't Arthur Trout's style. He told us to 'fight the good fight.' Maintaining the respect of his contemporaries and their players was of utmost importance to him. There were many games when Trout took me out. He resisted the temptation to humiliate an opponent by allowing our team to run up the score. During that last game of the '41 season, we were hot! We couldn't miss. Honestly, the crowd, the coaches, the players—everyone was caught up in the drama of that game against Vandalia."

That 1941 "Wonder Five" team won every regularly scheduled game that season, except for the loss to Taylorville. This prodigious talent, comprised of Eddleman, Harold Wesner, Jack Klosterman, Bob Michael and Bill Castleman, brought a great deal of media attention to Centralia and its sage basketball leader.

During 1941 postseason play, the Orphans experienced the agony of defeat. The 1941 state basketball tournament always will be remembered as a great disappointment to Eddleman and his "Wonder Five" teammates. Riding high on a fabulous winning streak, the Orphans were favored to win. It shocked *everyone* when Centralia lost to Morton of Cicero, a suburban Chicago school, by one point. Eddleman, who had paced Centralia through that nearly undefeated season, was held to 15 points. The 1941 Centralia starting lineup was touted as "the greatest team that never won the state tournament." The Orphans, who averaged 53.9 points a game and held their opposition to 23.8 points, ended the season 42-2.

Dike, and anyone who witnessed that infamous 1941 state contest, was heartbroken and disappointed after the game. Fans stood speechless in a state of shock. Players, eyes welled with tears, sat stunned in the locker room. Dike never forgot Coach Trout's postgame comments. "Listen, boys. The sun will come up again tomorrow. We'll eat baked beans, and life *will* go on. You know, I just might bring Eddleman back up here again next year if I can find a few boys who really want to play. Why, we might just win the whole thing!"

Port Gaston, Eddleman's best friend in high school, said Dike was somewhat superstitious about that 1941 state tournament loss. "As his close friend, Dike always asked me to hold this ruby ring he used to wear. His father had given it to him. I never missed a basketball game. After every contest, Dike would thank me for holding his 'lucky' ring. For some strange reason, Dike hadn't brought that ring to the 1941 state tournament in Champaign. There were many times he wondered if they had lost that game because he didn't have his 'lucky' ring with him that night."

The 1941 defeat did not dampen Eddleman's competitive spirit. Though Dike was the only returning senior on the 1942 Orphan basketball team, he and his teammates vowed to earn a trip to the playoffs in Champaign, Illinois, for another chance at that elusive state championship trophy.

Centralia fought an uphill battle to earn the basketball championship title in 1942. It accomplished this after strong fourth-quarter rallies during the tournament's semifinals and finals. With the exception of a game against West Frankfort, which the Orphans won 42-28, Centralia was forced to come from behind in its final two contests. In the Elite Eight, the Orphans beat Wood River by only two points.

Having beaten Freeport in regular season play 64-39, the Orphans were confident going into the semifinals. Leading 26-16 in the second quarter, the Orphans thought they had the game in the bag. However, Centralia's sloppy play and overconfidence allowed Freeport to narrow the margin to 27-20 at halftime.

After intermission, the Orphans missed their target frequently, allowing Freeport to tie the game at 32 by the end of the third quarter.

Merlin Belle, a strong Freeport player nicknamed "Ding Dong," tied the game at the third-quarter buzzer. With a strong showing by Belle in the fourth quarter, Freeport led 38-32 with only four minutes remaining.

Eddleman remembered the pressure. "We were getting emotional during that game. We'd already beaten this team by a considerable margin. Trout tried to help us focus during halftime. He said, 'Don't worry about playing in the final game boys until we get there.' "

With the clock ticking down, Eddleman threw up a long shot and missed. Fred Wham retrieved the rebound. After trading baskets, Freeport led 42-38.

This was Eddleman's kind of game. He played well under pressure. As time was running out, he drove down the sidelines. He faked his man out of position, leaped high into the air, shot and missed. Freeport rebounded, drove down the floor and also missed. With his feline agility, Eddleman jumped for a rebound. Dribbling slowly down the floor, Eddleman suddenly bounded forward, jumped straight into the air about 10 feet from the center line and sank a two-handed "set shot." When Centralia narrowed the margin to 42-40, the fans went wild.

After a steal by Farrell Robinson, Eddleman paused deep in the corner and aimed carefully. As his defender rushed toward him, Dike fired a long one. The ball rolled around the rim and out of the basket. "Ding Dong" Belle leaped up and touched the rim, forcing the official to signal two points for Centralia. This tied the game at 42.

With the crowd getting into the game, Freeport made a wild pass out of bounds. Centralia's Farrell Robinson drove the ball past the center line and shot from midcourt. Swish! Centralia led 44-42. With the final seconds ticking down, the Orphans stalled with the four corners until Eddleman was fouled. He put the free throw up and in. Then, utilizing a practiced technique, Farrell Robinson snagged another rebound. The semifinal game ended with Robinson dribbling around the back court, evading the frantic Freeport players. The Orphans won 45-43!

Orphan fans were used to these exciting finishes. After losing four starting seniors from the previous year, four new "horsemen" carried the torch. Farrell Robinson, Jim Seyler, Fred Wham and Freddie Pearson all stepped forward to contribute. At last, they had reached the pinnacle of their basketball season—the state tournament finals. "This group, on many occasions, disproved the one-man team theory in convincing style," Dike said.

Centralia found itself paired against a veritable powerhouse. The Paris Tigers came into the finals with 39 consecutive victories. They were heavily favored to beat the lowly Orphans. "We struggled into the final round of the tournament with the help of a horseshoe that traveled with the team all season," Dike said. More astute observers said the Orphans were successful because they never quit.

This game of games between Paris and Centralia ended Dike's high school basketball career in a blaze of glory. Many reporters rank it as one of the greatest Illinois state basketball games in the tournament's history.

Coming into this game as the only seasoned veteran, Dike gladly accepted the leadership role. As the minutes dwindled in each game that season, Dike came to the front like a war horse to help erase any deficit.

As the fourth quarter of the 1942 championship game between Centralia and Paris started, Eddleman had scored only four
points. With only five minutes left, Paris led by 13 points.
Eddleman, pale after a bout with strep throat and suffering from
blood blisters on both feet, rallied during the last minutes. With
55 seconds left, Eddleman was fouled as he shot. He tossed in
the first free throw and then the second with the infamous "Kiss
Shot," tying the score at 33. Seconds later, Dike leaped high to
grab a defensive rebound and dribbled the length of the court to
put up a short shot. Dike missed, but he grabbed his own rebound and put it in at the buzzer. The Orphans had captured the
third state tournament title for Centralia and Coach Trout! Pan-
demonium broke out in Huff Gym. Dike had made the trip to the
Sweet Sixteen three of his four years at Centralia. Remember—
there was only one state tournament then. Winning it all was the
ultimate reward for hours, days, weeks, even years of practice
and perseverance. Finally, the dream was reality. "At the buzzer, I
remember the crowd going crazy. After embracing Coach Trout,
I remember finding my favorite cheerleader and girlfriend Teddy.
It was an emotional high that has never been duplicated in my
career. Although I would go on to participate in the Rose Bowl,
the NCAA Final Four, the Olympic Games and the NBA, there was
no greater thrill for me in sports than winning the IHSA state
basketball championship in 1942," Dike said.

Bert Bertine wrote an article for the 1949 state basketball
tournament program, recalling the 1942 final game between
Centralia and Paris, in which he said: "The 1942 Centralia team
was only a remnant of that great 1941 team, but it still had Dike.
Winding up the most prolific scoring career in state annals,
Eddleman scored 12 points in that final period against Paris. He
shot long, he shot short, he rebounded like a demon and almost
single-handedly carried his team to the prize it should have won
the year before."

It was a sensational victory for the Cinderella team from
Southern Illinois. Although the accolades went to Eddleman for

his performance in the title game, Dike saluted Farrell Robinson, who pulled the Orphans through the sectional game with Mount Vernon. Eddleman, who had fouled out with four minutes remaining, had tears streaming down his face as Robinson scored the winning point, enabling the Orphans to advance to the state finals in Champaign.

Fate had brought together a group of exceptional young men, placed them under the guidance of an extraordinary teacher and allowed them to be nurtured in an environment steeped in tradition. Aided by the outstanding efforts of his talented teammates, Eddleman scored 2,702 points during his high school career, including 969 points his junior year. Eddleman scored in double figures 56 times. He tallied more than 40 points six times. During his senior year, Dike scored a game-high 48 points. Dike was named to three All-State basketball teams during his high school career.

Dike achieved these feats without the benefit of a three-point shot and despite being limited to four fouls a game. Dike's scoring stats are even more remarkable because some *teams* averaged only 30 points a game.

While Eddleman gained national recognition, he never lost the respect and admiration of his classmates as illustrated by this acrostic poem that was dedicated to Dike. It appeared in a November 1941 issue of the Centralia High School newspaper, *The Sphinx.*

"For No. 40"

Davy Jones was a sailor
and that is all good,
Isaac Newton worked problems
like all smart men should,
Kipling wrote stories —
but people want more
Eddleman, basketball and an outrageous score!

Everyone who has seen him
will always proclaim
Dike's one of the best
at the basketball game,
Dumping in baskets
from angles secluded
Leaving all in amazement,
the coaches included,
Ever dribbling the ball
the length of the floor,
Making a basket
and right back for more.
All will agree that
I'm talking with reason —
Nothing's been said
that he won't do this season!

—Merle Rogers

Friends said Eddleman's success never changed his down-to-earth personality. His classmates almost unanimously elected him student body president in 1941. At an assembly after the 1942 state basketball finals, Eddleman, as team captain, presented the first-place trophy to himself, as student body president. At the end of the assembly, the 1,200 students, led by the band, snake-danced their way through the town's business district, jamming traffic for the third time since Centralia won the state crown two nights before. The first celebration, lasting far into the night, began immediately after the championship game. The second celebration honored the team on its return Sunday afternoon from Champaign.

About 16,000 residents from Centralia and the surrounding area welcomed their heroes home. The team's yellow school bus was met 20 miles north of Centralia by an escort of delirious fans who cheered and honked their way back to the town that now was being called "Eddlemanville."

Lyall Smith, a correspondent for the *Chicago Daily News* who had come to Southern Illinois to report about Dike, made one of the most profound observations on that sunny spring afternoon. He wrote that at the rally there were speeches and cheers and more speeches by the coach and his players. "But while the crowd of hysterical fans pressed close around the team, there was a little lad standing over in the corner by the drug store all alone. He was dressed in the garb that Eddleman had standardized, a pair of blue denim overall trousers. He wasn't cheering but he was looking up at Eddleman with hero worship in his eyes. Somebody said he was a player on the local grade school team."

Idolized by young and old alike, Dike was a box office sensation! The games would be sold out wherever he played. Donald Drees, a reporter for the *St. Louis Star-Times,* said by 1942 an estimated 300,000 spectators had paid to see Eddleman play basketball. His magic on the court was credited with converting Centralia's $3,000 athletic deficit in 1941 to a $4,000 profit by 1942. This was amazing because it accumulated at 25 cents a ticket! Tournament games had fans paying scalpers $2 to $15 for a 50-cent ticket, the going price for standing room only. In 1941, several hundred people stood in line three hours in 20-degree weather to vie for 150 general admission tickets.

Opposing fans would arrive early just to get a glimpse of Dike as he got off the bus. Everybody wanted his autograph. Hundreds of admirers stood outside the locker room waiting for Dike. After a game, he signed as many autographs as he could before Coach Trout and his teammates pulled him back onto the bus.

During his senior year, Eddleman and his teammates played a 40-game regular season schedule. The team scores, including the state tournament games, remain impressive.

1941-42 CENTRALIA HIGH SCHOOL
BASKETBALL RECORD

Centralia	33	Sandoval	18
Centralia	39	Urbana	29
Centralia	32	Ashley	16
West Frankfort	40	Centralia	24
Centralia	47	Sandoval	18
Centralia	61	Springfield	18
Centralia	42	Decatur	29
Centralia	58	Vandalia	31
Carbondale	33	Centralia	28
Pontiac Tournament			
Centralia	42	Rushville	18
Centralia	42	West Aurora	27
Centralia	37	Rock Island	23
Centralia	45	Peoria Woodruff	41
Centralia	57	Herrin	23
Mt.Vernon	26	Centralia	23
Paris	47	Centralia	36
Centralia	36	Benton	26
Carbondale	35	Centralia	33
Centralia	45	Marion	32
Centralia	47	Harrisburg	27
Centralia	42	Vandalia	32
Centralia	32	West Frankfort	18
Mt.Vernon	32	Centralia	29
Centralia	52	Herrin	27
Centralia	50	Herrin	8
Centralia	36	Harrisburg	18
Centralia	79	Benton	29
Centralia	48	Marion	38
Centralia	45	Decatur	33
Centralia	62	Freeport	39
Sandoval Regional			
Centralia	69	Patoka	27
Centralia	54	Farina	14
Centralia	45	Salem	28
Centralia Sectional			
Centralia	63	Woodlawn	20
Centralia	64	Johnston City	39
Centralia	43	Mt.Vernon	42

State Tournament

Centralia	43	West Frankfort	28
Centralia	31	Wood River	29
Centralia	45	Freeport	42
Centralia	35	Paris	33

In the 156 Centralia basketball games in which Eddleman played, he averaged 17.3 points a game. He scored 328 points his freshman year, 571 points his sophomore year, 969 points his junior year and 834 points his senior year. An aggressive player who was the target of many flying fists and elbows, Dike fouled out many games because of the four-foul rule. If Dike didn't foul out, Trout usually took him out to avoid injury or routing.

The handsome boy with baby-blue eyes also excelled as one of the state's finest track stars. Dike won the state high jump championships in 1940, 1941 and 1942. He set a school record by jumping 6 feet, 6 3/4 inches, a Centralia record that stood until 1980. Dike's other track events included the quarter mile and the long jump.

"Much of my success as a high jumper can be attributed to Lowell Spurgeon," Dike said. "Lowell was an outstanding athlete at Centralia High School. I tried to emulate him as a youngster. Lowell participated in basketball, football and track. He continued his sports career at the University of Illinois where he became a starting halfback and captain of the U. of I. football team."

Dike's style of high jumping was known as the Western Roll. "If someone had tried to do the Fosbury Flop, it would have resulted in disqualification. In my day, a jumper's feet had to proceed his head over the bar," Dike said. "Raymond Lee, a University of Illinois Law School alumnus, has a home movie of me high-jumping in a college meet. He recently transferred it onto videotape for me. It's the only footage I have of my high jumping. I practiced it thousands of times! I would approach the bar from exactly 36 feet away at about a 45-degree angle. In the last 27 feet of my approach, I would increase my speed. At the point of takeoff, I would pull up with a lifting kick of my right leg from a slightly crouched position. I would then spring off the ground with my left leg as my arms would swing forward and up. Nearing the peak of my jump, I would extend my right leg as I drew up my left knee in preparation for a hitch kick. As I reached the lay-out position, I would hitch kick with my left leg so that my hips would be carried over the bar. My right arm would swing forward to draw my right shoulder across the bar while my left arm would snap downward. I'd throw my head and right arm back as I straightened my body to roll over the bar. My right leg would be pulled over the bar as my left leg continued kicking."

The hardest part was landing. "I would initially land on my left leg, my left knee and hand contacting the sand or sawdust a fraction of a second later (no foam pits—*Ouch*!). I used a combination hitch kick and Western Roll style that was all my own. If I had been a one-sport athlete, I may have been able to perfect the belly-roll style of jumping that was becoming popular at the time. But I never had an off-season, so I stayed with the style with which I was most comfortable."

Eddleman possessed a drive that has been exceeded by only a few athletes. In a 1941 article written by Jack Ryan, Coach Trout commented on Eddleman's spirit. "You know, he was operated on last summer. He had a knee fixed that he banged up before we made him quit playing football, and he had the surgeon work on his ankle. Now that ankle was hurt when he was running the 440-yard dash against Mount Vernon. He and this other boy were out in front by themselves, and this other boy went to pass Dike. He spiked Dike, ripping up his ankle something awful. Well, Dike won that race. He won it boiling mad and with his teeth gritted and the sweat standing out on his forehead. That's what I mean when I say he's a competitor."

A few weeks after that incident, Eddleman participated in the state high jump finals with a tightly taped ankle. Despite his injury, he won. Eddleman advanced to the state finals in the high jump all four years in high school, placing third his freshman year and winning first each of the other three.

Dike thrived on constant training and competition. He displayed an insatiable appetite for the physical realm. Many of his contemporaries said he never seemed to get enough of any sport. Track was no exception. Whether it was at the Wheaton, Paris or Urbana relays, he gave his all.

After his high school graduation, Eddleman participated in the Big Nine-Pacific Coast Conference Meet at Dyche Stadium in Evanston, Illinois. (Speaking of Dyche Stadium, Dad always laughs because people would ask him if they named Dyche Stadium after him. He jokingly would answer, "They sure did. Isn't it a shame they misspelled my name?") With Illinois High School Association permission, he performed in Evanston as an exhibition jumper, beating all the college contenders with a jump of 6-6 1/2.

By 1942, Dike's fame was skyrocketing! Fan letters, some addressed to "Eddlemanville", poured into Centralia. "Dike answered every one of them. No matter who they were from or what they said, he felt an obligation to respond," lifelong friend Dr. George Ross said. Packages from as far away as Chicago, 280 miles to the north, often would have "Yea, Eddleman" scribbled on them.

Hunting caps and plaid wool jackets became the rage in fashion as boys dressed like their favorite sports idol. When Dike wore his denim overalls rolled up just above his ankles, every boy in town did the same. When Trout insisted his players wear caps so they wouldn't catch cold, Dike donned a corduroy hunting cap. Suddenly, every apparel store in Centralia had a sign in the window saying it was sold out of "Eddleman Hats." Dike wore leather Lil' Abner style boots because they were the only pair of shoes he owned. Every youngster in town wanted a pair so they could look like Dike!

When Dike went to the movies, which was his favorite thing to do on Sunday afternoon, he would sit in the front row surrounded by youngsters. Although a shy and bashful young man, Dike loved the attention. Some would ask for his autograph; others would ask if they could touch him.

Not only was Eddleman a box office sensation, he also was a media darling! Because television had not made its formal debut, radio exercised one's imagination, and newspapers were filled with descriptive narrative. An example was printed in *The Bloomington Pantagraph* on January 3, 1941, in an article titled, "Pure Trying to Watch Eddleman," written by Simon Pure, a reporter covering the Pontiac Holiday Tournament.

> "I'm up here at the tournament to watch Eddleman who makes more baskets than the Navajo Indians. I missed his first three baskets because I was lighting a cigar. I missed the next three because I looked at my watch. I missed the next three because I glanced at the scoreboard. The score was nineteen to one and they took him out. I'm still here to see if I can catch him at work."

One reporter noted Eddleman's agility and speed in zigzagging down the basketball court. He referred to Dike's style as "jagged lightning." Still others called Dike the "Wizard of Swish" because many of his two-handed "Kiss Shots" never touched the rim on their way through the hoop.

Eddleman's high jumping expertise gave him an edge in basketball as he would leap high, reaching over his opponents' heads for rebounds and passes. Eddleman, an aggressive player, was also an innovator. In the Friday, January 30, 1942, edition of the *Chicago Daily News,* one sports writer told of Eddleman's ability to dunk the basketball!

> "In one game, Dike noted the opposing guards weren't checking him closely under the basket and asked a teammate to lob a pass over their heads. Dike caught this pass by leaping high into the air. At the top of the leap, he twisted around and dropped

the ball through the basket. Observers called it the greatest play ever seen on an Illinois court."

Tom Siler, in a January issue of *Sport* magazine, said, "In the spring of 1942, Eddleman was the best known, and most sought after high school athlete in America." Dike was the subject of cartoon drawings and caricatures in the *New York Sun* and the *San Antonio Express.* In the February 10, 1942, issue of *Look* magazine, Tom Mean wrote a seven-page spread on Centralia's athletic wonder titled "High School Hero." That same year, the *Chicago Daily News* ran a series of articles called "The Daily Doings of Dike."

Obviously, his family and his coach had made a sound decision in allowing Dike to attend classes and to participate in sports at Centralia High School. The road Eddleman chose provided him with the ride of a lifetime. Despite the separation from his family, the glory of his success soothed his pain, leaving no visible scars—except, of course, for the ones on his right knee and ankle.

CHAPTER 4

A CALL TO SERVICE DURING WWII

With the national exposure Dike was receiving, there was much speculation about where he would attend college. In the spring of 1942, he still was being recruited by major universities from across the country. Would he choose Indiana University, Coach Trout's alma mater? Since he had spent six weeks in Ann Arbor, Michigan, after his knee surgery, would he head north in his pursuit of higher education? Even Notre Dame was knocking at the door. By the middle of his senior year in high school, Eddleman was being recruited by colleges from the South, West and Midwest, including Northwestern, Purdue, Alabama, Kentucky, Tennessee and Texas. All were begging him to attend. Coach Trout refused to advise him.

The spring of 1942 was unsettled. The attack on Pearl Harbor had surprised and shocked the United States, plunging the country into war in distant parts of the world. Despite this occurrence, time still could be found to worry about the paramount sports question of the day. Where was Dike Eddleman, touted as "the nation's number one prep athlete," going to attend college? Dike took his time before committing.

In December 1941, Dike and the other All-State football players were invited to a banquet in Champaign, Illinois, that was
sponsored by the *News-Gazette.* Governor Dwight Green, the
guest speaker, publicly recognized Eddleman. He said he hoped
the youth would attend the University of Illinois. "We Dwights
have to stick together," Green said. In March, their paths crossed
again when Green was the featured speaker at the Centralia High
School athletic banquet honoring the 1942 state basketball
champs. In his speech, Green said the Centralia-Paris basketball
game would be remembered as one of the greatest games in Illinois sports history, again praising Eddleman.

After the banquet, R. J. Branson, Centralia's state representative, arranged a conference between Dike and Green in Springfield because rumors were circulating that Eddleman might attend an out-of-state university. The governor must have done a
good job promoting the state because shortly after this meeting
Eddleman enrolled at the University of Illinois in Champaign-Urbana. The high school prep star enthusiastically turned in his
red-and-white Orphan uniforms for the orange-and-blue ones of
the Fighting Illini. Dike looked forward to playing in Huff Gymnasium, an accessible location where his family and friends could
travel to watch him play. Huff held great memories for Dike, and
he loved playing there. With an athletic scholarship in hand, Dike
headed to Champaign-Urbana after spending the summer at Culver Military Academy in Indiana.

When asked why he chose Illinois, Dike said, "Many of those
1941 All-State football players agreed to come to Illinois. As a
matter of fact, more than a third of that All-State squad ended up
going there. Governor Green sold me on the idea that the state's
premier athletes should attend the state's best educational institution. Another thing that influenced my decision was the fact
that some schools guaranteed good grades. Some even came right
out and said they would let you miss classes. I didn't make very
good grades my first two years in high school, but Coach Trout
warned me that I couldn't go to college if I neglected my school

work. So I got busy and studied. I remember Coach Doug Mills telling me I'd have to work for what I got at Illinois, especially in the classroom. That was fine with me. One of the reasons I came to Illinois was to prove I had what it took academically as well as athletically."

During his freshman year at Illinois, Dike found the competition challenging. His arrival in the fall of 1942 coincided with an influx of talented basketball and gridiron prep stars. The talk of the campus and the country was a sensational group of sharpshooters called the Whiz Kids, who included Art Methisen, Ken Menke, Andy Phillip, Jack Smiley and Gene Vance. Eddleman enjoyed college life. Dike joined friends from the Wham and Corbell families from Centralia in pledging the Sigma Chi social fraternity. Dike joined the freshman football team, at the coaxing of track coach Leo Johnson, because the team needed a kicker. He also joined the basketball and track teams.

In January 1943, after only one semester at the University of Illinois, Eddleman's college career abruptly was put on hold. Like so many other young men, Dike was called to military duty. When he enrolled in his first-semester classes at the university, Eddleman signed up for the ROTC program. Dike was told that by doing this he would be guaranteed of staying in school for the year. One day, as Dike walked through the Armory, he saw a group of students gathered around a bulletin board. On it was posted a list of the most recent draftees. There, at the top of the list and much to his surprise, appeared the name Thomas D. Eddleman. Dike soon received a letter from Uncle Sam saying he had been drafted into the Army Air Corps. His induction papers ordered him to report to a base near Chicago. After a quick trip home to Centralia on the Illinois Central to get his belongings and say his goodbyes, Dike headed north to Fort Sheridan.

On the night before his induction, Dike entered the Illinois Tech Relays and jumped 6-6 for first place, cinching a letter at Illinois. After arriving at Fort Sheridan, Dike was given permission to participate in the *Chicago Daily News* Relays, an indoor track meet that was held at Chicago Stadium. Dike participated in this meet only two days after his induction. Dike beat the nation's best jumper, Dave Albritton, a world-class Olympic high jumper. Eddleman won the *Chicago Daily News* Relays again in 1945 for Wright Patterson Field in Ohio and in 1946 and 1948 for the University of Illinois.

Eddleman earned a letter for his performance in the Illinois Tech Relays in 1943 because, as a result of the war, the Big Nine Conference had ruled freshmen eligible for varsity competition. With permission from the Big Nine commissioner, the conference later agreed to waive Dike's one-meet appearance, let him keep his letter and not count it as a season of eligibility. This ruling was not a privilege for Eddleman. The reason he could compete later, without shortening his athletic career, was because the Big Nine granted servicemen an extra season of eligibility provided it was used by June 1946. The track letter Eddleman earned in 1943, incidentally, was the first one awarded to an Illinois freshman in 37 years—just another feat in a record-breaking career. Dike earned five track letters at Illinois.

In 1943, the university record for all-around performance by an athlete was nine letters held jointly by Burt Ingwersen, Illini football line coach who competed from 1918-20; George Fencl, an Illini sports star in the early 1930s; and Web Henry, a Sigma Chi athletic standout who played from 1935-37. With the service interrupting his collegiate career, Eddleman had no idea if or when he would return to his beloved campus. Earning more varsity letters was not a priority.

At Fort Sheridan, Eddleman felt right at home being assigned to bunk number 40. Although the war temporarily interrupted Eddleman's athletic endeavors at Illinois, the Army provided plenty of opportunities for him to compete in basketball, football and track. Ten days after arriving at Fort Sheridan, Dike was reassigned. Dike said he and 12 others were told they were being shipped out, but they weren't told where they were going or why. He and the others were anxious and afraid as they boarded the train to an unknown destination. Dike said the train stopped somewhere in Alabama. Dike's orders were changed, and he was assigned to Miami Beach, Florida. He never knew what happened to those other 12 men. He never saw them again.

Dike was wearing a wool khaki Army dress uniform when he received the new orders to report to Florida. "To this day, I remember that I almost died from heat exhaustion when I got off the train. I was wearing that wool uniform and carrying my two duffel bags. It must have been 100 degrees the day I arrived in Miami. What a deal!"

At Miami Beach Air Force Base, Dike, 20, was assigned as a Physical Trainer, i.e., P.T. Dike and the other P.T.s led about 50,000 young cadets in calisthenics on the beach with the help of loud-speakers. Eddleman said, "Some would jokingly refer to this tropical location as the site of the Battle of Biscayne Bay." Fortunately, the most dangerous action he encountered during the war was when he fractured his right ankle during a beach volleyball game.

Many of Eddleman's friends were sent to exotic locations. "Flip" Seely takes credit for spreading Dike's fame as far away as Okinawa. When the Japanese surrendered and World War II ended, "Flip" was stationed there with the Navy. "Flip" spent a lot of time ashore at a little recreational area where there was a dirt basketball court. One of his buddies, Carl Lloyd, was a good basketball player from Indiana who later made the starting five at Notre Dame. "Flip" did a lot of bragging about Dike. Carl kidded him about it, claiming that nobody outside of Centralia ever heard of Dike. Carl knew better, of course, but it became a subject of running banter between them.

"Flip" finally got a brainstorm about how to put Carl in his place. "Flip" quietly coaxed a couple of Japanese ex-POWs over to the basketball court and introduced them to the game—just enough so they occasionally could get the ball through the hoop. "Flip" managed to explain to them that the custom in America was that every time a player made a basket, he shouted "Eddleman," and the player with the most "Eddlemans" won. "Flip" then casually induced Carl over to the court to witness a demonstration of how far Dike's fame had spread. After two or three happy shouts of "Eddleman" (which, having trouble with their "Ls", they pronounced "Edduramon"), they had a good laugh. Carl realized then that "Flip" was not one to be trifled with about Dike. Carl never brought up Dike's name again. Dike was glad that "Flip" returned safely at the war's end to relay this amusing anecdote.

While stationed in Miami Beach, Eddleman played in a "five by five" basketball league. He has fond memories of a special player-coach, Bruce Hale. Hale was an excellent leader who played at Santa Clara College. Dike said Hale, Rick Barry's father-in-law, was one of the best players he faced in service ball. Another All-America player whom Dike grew to respect through service league play was an Illinois Sigma Chi, Bill Hapac. Although they attended Illinois, Eddleman did not become friends with Hapac until their assignment in Miami. After 18 months in Florida, Eddleman was sent to Scott Field near Belleville, Illinois.

While at Scott Field, Dike was recruited by Chuck Taylor, former star for the original New York Celtics. Eddleman soon transferred to Wright-Patterson Field in Dayton, Ohio, where he continued his basketball career for the Air Tec Kittyhawk Flyers, one of the nation's greatest service quintets. Taylor, a commissioned colonel in the Army and a lieutenant in the Navy whose later claim to fame was his affiliation with Converse tennis shoes, coached the Flyers. Taylor said, "Eddleman is a greater basketball player right now than Hank Luisetti, the famous Stanford player. Give him three more years at the University of Illinois and he'll make you forget the names of a lot of other guys who have played basketball in this country."

Dike's decision to transfer from Scott Field to Wright-Patterson was easy. "My superior at Scott Field called me into his office and asked me if I wanted to go to Wright Field and play for the Kittyhawk Flyers or go to the infantry. I caught up with the Air Tec basketball team in Evansville, Indiana, where they were on the road playing," Dike said.

Publicized as "a Whiz Kid who hadn't had a chance to whiz," Eddleman played against teams at other bases—even Chanute Field in Rantoul, Illinois. The Flyers played against the Illini (who hailed such players as Jack Burmeister and Chick Doster) and won! While playing with the Flyers, Eddleman was named twice to the College All-Star Team, which was comprised of the country's best college basketball players.

The money generated by the Flyers' games was donated to General Jimmy Doolittle's wife. She gave it to her favorite charity via the Army Air Corps Relief Fund. The Flyers traveled from California to Texas to New York. One particularly memorable game for Dike was when the Flyers beat the Harlem Globetrotters in 1945.

During another unforgettable game in Los Angeles, Eddleman's team saw a woman in the locker room. During halftime of a game against 20th-Century Fox, Lucille Ball visited with his team. "She was stunning," Dike said. "She told several jokes and really seemed excited about the game. On her way out of the dressing room, she smacked me on the butt and said, 'Good luck, honey!' My teammates got a big kick out of that! I think she inspired us to win the game!"

By 1946, Eddleman had been promoted to sergeant. The Flyers, the nation's top service team, continued to play exhibition games. One of Dike's favorite Flyer games was his farewell appearance against Fort Sheridan on February 12, 1946. The match-up rekindled an old prep rivalry between Eddleman and defensive starter Dick Foley of Paris, Illinois. Played at Centralia in Trout Gym, the teams performed for a packed house of "Eddlemaniacs" who were treated to another Eddleman victory.

During his three-year service stint, Dike kept in shape participating in basketball and track. On June 28, 1944, at the fifth

annual Scott Field track and field meet, Eddleman made headlines as a one-man team. He set two records: one for high-jumping 6-6 1/8 and the other for broad jumping 22 feet. Dike also
placed second in the triple jump and quarter mile and fifth in the
shot put. Eddleman, the lone participant from his unit, scored 30
points for Scott Field. The meet was won by the Evanston Athletic Club, whose team scored 72 points.

Eddleman was worried that his high-jumping form would
suffer because most bases had only outdoor track facilities. At
Wright Field, he didn't even have a coach. Dike had to hitchhike
to a neighboring high school 10 miles away to practice. After his
day's work was completed on the base, he practiced high jumping for an hour.

By mid-1946, the war had taken its toll. The lives of the
young athletes who had been inducted into the armed forces
from colleges across the country were changed forever. Eddleman
was one of the lucky ones who made a successful transition from
military to college life. Eddleman said, "You had guys who returned to college after having been shot at. They came home
more mature and more serious. Alex Agase must have been 26
or 27 years old by the time he returned to campus. Many left the
college setting as young boys but returned as grown men who
had seen or experienced the atrocities of war. Many players found
it difficult to regain their athletic rhythm, but those who returned
were the lucky ones."

Twenty-five Illinois lettermen died during World War II. A
Gold Star List of Illini was released naming those lettermen who
were killed in the line of duty. The number of Illini athletes who
served in the armed forces numbered in the thousands. Eddleman
said several talented athletes were among the casualties. There
were football standouts Tony Butkovich, Richard Good, Robert
Ingle, James McDonald, Paul Milosevich and George Rettinger.
Another friend lost in the war was basketball player Bob Rich-
mond.

With peace came many postwar dreams for Illinois coaches, athletes and fans. Would those dreams come true? No one knew for sure. Of the four Whiz Kids who still had a year of eligibility—Andy Phillip, Gene Vance, Ken Menke and Jack Smiley—all said they planned to return to Illinois. With Phillip in the Marines and the other three in the Army, there was no guarantee they would be discharged at the same time. Menke and Smiley had acquired more combat points than Vance. The Marines had no such point system for release. A big question for the Illini basketball program was whether the Whiz Kids would play together again.

If all the basketball players who left Illinois returned together, the Illini would have a tremendous lineup. Adding names such as Dike Eddleman, Junior Kirk, Voe Van Hooreweghe, Fred Green, Chet Strumillo, Dick Foley, John Orr, Howie Judson and Walt Kersulis to those of the Whiz Kids, the prospects of producing a powerhouse were undeniable.

Coach Ray Eliot predicted an equally promising varsity football team. He drew up a list of 125 undergraduate players who had left for the service since 1942. All 125 had one or more years of eligibility remaining. Alex Agase, an All-America guard, returned with a year to play. Sam Zatkoff, a Navy specialist, returned for three more years of football. Julie Rykovich, who attended Illinois as a freshman but had played a year at Notre Dame, was coming back. Frank Bauman and Joe Buscemi, who played as ends at Illinois in 1942, also returned with eligibility after playing at Purdue in the Marine program.

Track also had its returning aces: Bob Rehberg, Leroy Vranek, Clarence Dunn, Bob Seib, Buddy Young, Dike and many others.

Eddleman said about 300 men showed up for football tryouts. Athletic Director Doug Mills expanded the intramural program because of the interest. There was even a lightweight football team for men weighing less than 150 pounds. This team played intercollegiate games with a full-time staff of coaches.

After returning to the University of Illinois as a second-semester freshman in the spring of 1946, Eddleman was issued his Fighting Illini athletic uniforms. Discharged from the Army on Friday, February 15, 1946, Eddleman was entered by track coach Leo Johnson in a track meet with Ohio State the next day. Arriving at the Ohio State campus hours after his discharge, Dike participated in the meet, which began at 1:30 p.m.

Basketball coach Doug Mills scheduled Dike to see action in the next home game against Wisconsin that following Monday night. Able to practice only once with the team, Eddleman worked right in because he knew the offense. Eager to play both sports, Dike was at the mercy of Johnson and Mills. Obviously, each coach wanted to stake his claim to Eddleman. It was difficult when basketball games and track meets conflicted. Doug Mills was not flexible, but he felt pressure to keep a talent such as Eddleman on the team.

Returning to campus as a mature athlete, Eddleman soon emerged as a collegiate champion because he had what it took to be a winner. Dike continued to be successful because he possessed a strong body, a deep affection for sports and the ability to stay relaxed during constant training. With a fierce determination to excel and the war years behind him, Eddleman, tanned and in top condition from his travels with the Flyers, still was determined to earn his college degree.

CHAPTER 5

DIKE'S MARRIAGE TO HIS HIGH SCHOOL SWEETHEART

With all this talk about a 6-3 blue-eyed, bronzed Adonis, what about the women in his life? There was only one girl who captured Eddleman's attention, and their relationship turned out to be a classic case of love at first sight.

Dike met his high school sweetheart in Trout Gym. Because of the bolstered economy in Centralia, the high school's enrollment grew from 200 students in the 1920s to about 1,200 students by the late 1930s. One of those 1,200 students enrolled at Centralia in 1939 was a pretty, petite brunette named Teddy Georgia Townsley. According to Marjorie (Oldham) Hoyt, Teddy's closest friend in high school, "Dike fell in love with Teddy, and there was never any question in his mind that she was the one for him. Other girls were crazy about him and would do just about anything to get him. I felt so lucky being 'the friend of the friend'. Teddy was the peppy cheer-leader, and Dike was the star athlete. High school was such fun. We had many wonderful times together! Since most of our teachers are gone now, I guess it wouldn't hurt to confess how I used to be a 'lookout' over the lunch hour so that Teddy and Dike could smooch in the halls. Dike's practice schedule didn't leave much time for them to be together."

Teddy was one of two daughters born to Neva Florence Townsley. Teddy and her older sister, Betty, grew up at 1111 E. Third St. with their grandparents, Mr. and Mrs. Charles Posten. Their mother, Neva, worked as a buyer for infants' and children's wear in department stores in Chicago, Milwaukee and Washington, D.C. Neva was a successful businesswoman, having created the "chubby line" for children.

With only two years' age difference, Teddy and Betty appeared to be twins, sharing the same delicate features and diminutive builds. They always were dressed in the latest fashions and often were asked to model in Chicago and St. Louis because of their mother's career.

The Posten home was only two blocks from the high school but nearly two miles from the Eddleman house, which was located across town. "When we first started seeing each other, Dike used to run over to my house, and we'd sit on the porch talking for hours; then he'd run back home. Maybe that's one reason he kept in such good shape. It was a long way. Hot or cold, rain or shine, he'd run back and forth—always allowing enough time to get home by Coach Trout's curfew," Teddy said.

Teddy's grandmother was not interested in sports, but she liked Dike because she thought he was a good boy. Teddy said her grandmother used to make fruitcake every Christmas for Dike. She insisted that Dike have a huge piece. To be polite, Dike raved about how good it was. Years later, Dike confided that he hated fruitcake. Dike said he slipped the piece into his pocket and threw it as far as he could on his way home.

Teddy knew sports was the most important thing in Dike's life. Consequently, she accepted Coach Trout's rules as law. Teddy was Coach Trout's neighbor, living only two blocks from him. Every noon, she would walk softly behind him on her way home for lunch. During the years Teddy and Dike dated, her presence was acknowledged by the coach only once. It was one day after a home basketball game. The dean of women, Mrs. Jennings, called

Teddy into her office to tell her that Coach Trout had asked that she not turn flips and cheer so close to the team. The coach obviously had caught the sparks flying between Teddy and Dike.

Trout insisted on a rigorous training program that probably would cause today's youth to quit on the first day of practice. Under the Trout regime, a player followed the rules or he was gone. Bedtime was 9:30 p.m. unless a tournament game was being played. Then it was 8 p.m. sharp! Proper diet was encouraged, too. Eddleman's pregame meal consisted of a big glass of orange juice. The team, financially flush during the oil boom, was treated to steak dinners with all the trimmings after each game. Bill Davies said Dike had a fabulous appetite. After eating T-bone steaks for dinner, he topped it off with a half-gallon of ice cream for dessert.

Practice began with drills from 6:45-8:15 a.m. five days a week. If a player didn't practice, he didn't play. Dike said it wasn't something players felt obligated to do. "We loved it because we were seeking to perfect our 'natural talents' as Trout reminded us." Morning practices were only the beginning of a day's drills. At noon, the Orphans practiced for 40 minutes, and an after-school session lasted from 3:30-5:30 p.m. The team worked out about four hours daily.

With his rigorous training schedule, Dike had time for only one date each weekend with Teddy. In a series of articles in the *St. Louis Star-Times* in 1942 written by Donald H. Drees titled "The Amazing Dwight Eddleman, Centralia Blitzkrieg Cager," Dike addressed his dating philosophy. "I only have about 10 years for basketball and other athletic competitions. I have the rest of my life for girls. I limit my dating to one night each weekend. Just so I won't go stale!"

With Teddy as a cheerleader, sports was the common denominator that bonded their friendship. This shared passion has solidified their relationship throughout the years. Teddy always has supported her best friend's hopes and dreams. She remains loyal, generous, intelligent and funny. Their courtship continued through high school, Dike's first semester of college and his induction into the Army. Teddy was always there, waiting patiently. She never complained because Dike, she claimed, "was worth waiting for."

It wasn't easy when Dike left high school for college. Teddy still had a year to go. When Teddy graduated from high school, she planned to attend the University of Illinois. However, the war interfered, and Dike went off to the service. Teddy, thinking the war would last only a year or so, decided to attend Layton Art School in Milwaukee. She planned to enroll at the U. of I. when Dike returned.

During the summer of 1944 while on leave from the Army, Dike visited Rhinelander, Wisconsin, where Teddy was vacationing with her mother at the family cottage. Teddy spent many happy summers there, but this was a summer she will never forget. During this visit, while Teddy and Dike were rowing on the lake, he proposed to her. "I jumped up and hugged him, almost tipping over the boat," Teddy said. Even though Dike still was serving in the Army, a December wedding was planned.

On December 25, 1945, Teddy became Dike's bride in a candlelight ceremony at the First Christian Church in Centralia. The wedding was *the* social event of the season. As World War II came to an end, gala social gatherings were uncommon. Since this was no ordinary couple, a simple ceremony was out of the question.

Fifteen white fir trees were placed at the front of the sanctuary. Gold candelabra with white tapered candles lighted the church, which was decorated with a "White Christmas" theme. Among the musical selections sung at the wedding was "The Sweetheart of Sigma Chi." The bride entered the church on the arm of her grandfather, Charles Posten, to the strains of the Lohengrin wedding march.

Mrs. James Randolph Earle, the bride's sister, was the matron of honor, and Marjorie Oldham, Helen Hasemeir, Joyce Pfeffer and Mary Ann Jensen were bridesmaids. Dressed in white, the attendants carried white net muffs covered with red American Beauty roses. The bride was a classic, wearing a full-length white Skinner satin wedding gown styled with a fitted bodice, carved scalloped neckline and long pointed sleeves. Teddy had a full-length circular veil of silk imported illusion that fell from a crystallized orange blossom tiara. The bride carried three white orchids on a small white Bible.

The groom looked dashing in his United States Army Air Corps dress uniform. He was attended by Bob Michael as best man and Jack Klosterman, James Earle, Bill Wilson, Stanley Wilson, Robert Liles and Lieutenant Phillip Corbell as ushers.

A reception, held in the Jade Room at the Langenfeld Hotel immediately after the ceremony, included music by the Reveliers. A gorgeous three-tiered cake was created for the couple. Teddy said ration stamps were given to her by friends so enough sugar could be purchased for the cake.

"A highlight of our wedding," said Teddy, "was the ring Dike gave me. The first-place medals from the *Chicago Daily News* Relays had a small diamond in each of them. Dike had the stones removed from the medals and put in a wedding band for me."

The young bride left for her honeymoon wearing a cherry red wool suit. She also wore a beaver coat with a matching hat that her mother had given her. After a short weekend trip to St. Louis, the Eddlemans made their home in Dayton, Ohio, at Wright-Patterson Air Force Base. Life in the service was brief for the newlyweds.

CHAPTER 6

THE EMERGENCE OF A COLLEGIATE CHAMPION: 1946-1948

In February 1946, as a mature 23-year-old, Eddleman had reached his prime and was eligible to compete that semester because the Big Nine had granted servicemen that extra season of eligibility. Dike returned to Illinois as a newlywed in time to play in the last basketball game of the 1946 season, perform as an outstanding high jumper on the Illini's Big Nine and National Collegiate Athletic Association championship track team and seek a starting position in football by going out for spring practice.

An abundance of ex-servicemen vied for playing time on Coach Ray Eliot's 1946 University of Illinois football team. Sam Zatkoff, who completed only one semester before his military induction, was admitted to the university as a second-semester freshman at age 26. Paul Patterson, Buddy Young and Vern Seliger were teammates on the Fleet City Navy Team, which was crowned service champions in 1945. Other service players included: Ruck Steger, who played fullback with the Honolulu Army All-Stars; Tom Gallagher, who played for the Air Force Bombers; Julie Rykovich, who was a member of the Pacific Marine All-Stars; and Bill Huber, who had been selected to three All-Star teams while playing for the Army in Texas. Although the war interrupted their tenures at various colleges, many players returned to campus with a wealth of playing experience and All-Star honors to their credit.

While enrolled at the University of Illinois in 1946, one might say there were really three Dike Eddlemans in one. There was the 6-3, 190-pounder who played right halfback and punter; the 185-pounder who gained All-America basketball fame; and the 180-pounder who flew over the high jump crossbar with ease. Dike was a serious, modest and tireless athletic machine who remained in constant training.

Considering Eddleman's financial status, athletic practices were one of the few things he could afford to do. Returning to college on the G.I. Bill, Teddy and Dike received $88 a month— plus Dike's tuition and fees. Teddy obtained a secretarial job in Coach Eliot's office and later was given the responsibility of preparing the Illini Union payroll.

That spring, the couple moved into an apartment across from Newman Hall on Chalmers Street. Their second residence was the three-story Bresee apartment house on California Street. Teddy said their second apartment housed other athletes and their wives. Ruck and Joan Steger lived on the first floor; Teddy and Dike resided on the second floor; and Denny Bassett and his wife occupied the third floor. Teddy sometimes pounded on the porch floor signaling Ruck Steger to stop playing his guitar late at night.

Their kitchen had a small refrigerator. The Eddlemans loved having get-togethers on weekends. Stag beer in large bottles was one of Dike's favorite weekend beverages. Because their refrigerator was small, they would fill the bathtub with ice to chill the beer bottles. Teddy said the tub got a thorough cleaning every weekend because Dike had to scrape the Stag labels off the side of the tub the morning after every party.

The Eddlemans were lucky enough to own a car, a dark blue Ford convertible that had a leaky roof. Teddy figured out a clever solution to this problem. She kept an old umbrella under the front seat that she unfolded *inside* the car whenever the couple had to drive in the rain.

Needing extra money, Dike took various jobs on campus such as painting numerals on the stadium seats. One summer, he had an interesting job working for Al Klingel, University of Illinois swim coach, at one of his camps. One of Dike's responsibilities was to pick up and deliver children to and from the camp in a station wagon. One of his afternoon deliveries turned disastrous when Dike shut one of the camper's fingers in the car door. Happily, the young camper never held any animosity toward Dike or the University of Illinois. The boy whose finger was smashed that day happened to be Clint Atkins, an outstanding Illinois alumnus who generously donated funds for the Atkins Tennis Center on the U. of I. campus.

One of Dike's most important goals was to earn a degree from Illinois. He was the first member of his family to attend college, and, just as in sports, he was driven to succeed at this goal. He enrolled as a physical education major with a biology minor. Despite a rigorous daily schedule, Dike attended and enjoyed his undergraduate courses. He remembered Dr. Walter Elhardt's anatomy class. Doc Elhardt, as Eddleman affectionately called him, was a great booster of the Illini athletic program. Doc referred to his Physiology 234 students as his "All-America Class" because there were so many students enrolled in it who had achieved that status. "Doc Elhardt spent many extra hours tutoring and helping athletes like myself who had trouble keeping up with labs due to demanding practice and performance schedules," Dike said.

In the 1940s, the U. of I. had one of the most prestigious physical education departments in the country. Leading the school in research was the renowned Dr. Thomas Cureton. Dike said he would duck down hallways trying to avoid one of Dr. Cureton's stress tests. "Placing champion-caliber athletes on treadmills and running them to the point of exhaustion was one of Dr. Cureton's favorite projects. Now I look back and understand how important his contributions were. He was truly the 'Father of Fitness.'"

Although Dike's experiences at the U. of I. sound like the proverbial "carefree college days," nothing is further from the truth. He was awarded his starting positions because of persistence and perseverance. He wasn't given good grades; he earned them. He was no longer under the protective wing of father-figure Coach Arthur Trout. In fact, Coach Doug Mills seemed to hold a grudge against Dike, making his participation in three sports more difficult. Although Eddleman had been one of the most highly publicized athletes in the nation, he did not expect special treatment. He never demanded or requested special favors. However, with offers from countless other institutions, it must have crossed his mind how different his career could have been if he had chosen to go elsewhere. Being a man who follows through with his commitments, Dike continued working for Coach Mills, trying to win his favor. Eddleman quoted a wonderful poem by Edwin Markham that describes the way he handled Mills: "He drew a circle that shut me out. Heretic, rebel, a thing to flout. But love and I had the wit to win. We drew a circle that took him in."

Although it was a difficult assignment in politics and coordination, the basketball, football and track coaches at Illinois decided to share Eddleman's multiple athletic talents. As the next three years would prove, this was a shrewd administrative decision on behalf of the University of Illinois athletic department.

SPRING OF 1946

In the spring of 1946, Eddleman found himself among an influx of extremely talented student-athletes returning to college after having been scattered throughout the world by Uncle Sam.

The competition was tough. Eddleman found himself "riding the pine" in basketball, playing as a reserve with the nationally renowned "Whiz Kids." Ending the 1946 season with a 14-6 record, the famed "Whiz Kids" had lost much of their prewar prowess.

In football, Eddleman was a third-string right halfback. In *Sport Life* magazine, Dike was quoted after answering one of his fellow reserves who was complaining bitterly that they deserved a better fate than sitting on the bench. "What are you griping about? Aren't we out here for the fun of it? What difference does it make which team we're on?" On that philosophical note, Dike made his postwar debut, soon to become the Illini's greatest all-around everything. Refusing to be discouraged by reserve status in basketball and football, Dike remained optimistic about his sports career.

His track success rekindled his desire and determination. Under Coach Leo Johnson, Dike set a record of 6-7 1/8 in the high jump at the Big Nine Indoor Track competition. Dike went down in the record books as the only freshman to earn points in a Big Nine track meet.

The Fighting Illini track team had a superb season in 1946 when it did not lose a meet. A galaxy of colorful stars, breaking a myriad of records, would be the legacy of that great 1946 team. Sports history was made as Coach Johnson wisely split up his track squad for the Drake and the Penn relays, resulting in a first-place finish in both meets. Johnson and his class of superb track stars scored victories over Ohio State in the Big Nine meet, Wisconsin in the Central Collegiate meet and Southern California in the NCAA meet. Promoting perseverance and sportsmanship, Johnson skillfully led the Illini track men to become the nation's top-ranked team.

Eddleman's teammates included: Herb McKenley, world-class sprinter; Bob Rehberg, record-holding distance runner; John and Vic Twomey, standouts in the two-mile run; and Bob Richards and captain Bob Phelps, champion pole-vaulters. Eddleman said a sense of team spirit and camaraderie existed among his track teammates.

Meet after meet, records fell. The Illini traveled to West Point for a four-way contest with Army, Dartmouth and Columbia. The Illini emerged winners, 80-48. A week later, Illinois continued its record-breaking rampage with a 90-32 trouncing of visiting Purdue.

The Orange and Blue men were on their way to a national crown when they taught Michigan a lesson, winning a meet 80-42. In that contest, the Illini finished first in every running event, aced the pole vault and won the high jump and broad jump thanks to Eddleman. Preparing for the Western Conference Meet, Illinois beat a strong Minnesota squad, 75-41, taking nine firsts and winning all the dashes and the mile run.

The Big Nine track finals on June 1, 1946, proved no exception for this group. Despite chilly and cloudy conditions, Herb McKenley set a world record in the 440 in 46.2 seconds. The Illini took the conference crown with 66 3/4 points, more than double the total of their nearest rival, Ohio State.

Two weeks after the Big Nine meet, Illinois traveled to Milwaukee for the Central Collegiate track meet. With many reserves competing, the Illini squad scored three times as many points as the second-place finishers from Wisconsin.

The NCAA meet was a two-team duel between Illinois and Southern California. The enthused Trojan fans were in for a disappointment. Some of the 14,000 spectators anticipated a close race. However, the Illini scored 78 points to the Trojans' 43. By meet's end, the Illini had beaten the Trojans in every event but two.

Raymond Lee, prominent attorney who was a law student on the Champaign-Urbana campus, said, "I used to walk over to the stadium after classes to watch the track boys. Norm Wasser, a shot putter, was the leader of my navy service school company at Bainbridge, Maryland. I would go over and visit with him. Also, I got to watch Bob Richards and Dike. It was exhilarating just watching them practice. You knew many of them were destined for greatness because of their incredible talent." This was a remarkable period for Illini track and field.

1946-47

As fall 1946 arrived, Coach Ray Eliot's football team came under pressure to perform to the standards of their glowing press releases. There was a great deal of anticipation concerning All-Americas Julie Rykovich and Alex Agase, the lightning-fast Buddy Young and sure-footed punter Dike Eddleman. These standouts along with Perry Moss, Bill Huber, Bill Franks, John Wrenn, Tom Stewart, Art Dufelmeier, Paul Patterson and Jim Valek made the Illini football programs read like a list from *Who's Who in Football*. In the season opener, Illinois trounced Pittsburgh 33-7.

A record 75,000 fans attended the Illini's game against Notre Dame at Memorial Stadium. Fans hoped the Illini would emerge with their first victory over the Fighting Irish. Although Notre Dame won 26-6, the two colleges continued to become giants that season. Notre Dame was the top team in the nation, and Illinois became the Western Conference champions.

Next on the schedule was Purdue. Coming off the Notre Dame defeat, Illinois was ready to play. The Illini were able to score at will en route to a 43-7 victory. This game was a turning point for the rest of the season, due in large part to Eddleman's punting. Dike finished the Purdue game with an incredible average of 54 yards a punt. Time after time, Dike put Purdue in such terrible field position that Illinois touchdowns were the result. Dike also ran for the longest carry of the day—56 yards for a touchdown.

Indiana, the defending champion, handed the Illini a 14-7 defeat as Illinois' collection of veterans had not yet become a well-oiled machine. There was a great deal of pessimism concerning Illinois' hopes for a conference title.

Homecoming Saturday in 1946 saw a capacity crowd fill Memorial Stadium to witness a 27-21 upset of Wisconsin. Buddy Young demonstrated his speed for many long gains; Perry Moss executed stellar passing skills; and Julie Rykovich found his fierceness from the past.

Dike's enthusiasm to excel was obvious. Gene Shalit, a former *Daily Illini* reporter now a movie critic on NBC's "Today" show, wrote an article about Dike prior to the Michigan game. He wrote, "Yesterday afternoon, before the Illini took to the rails for Michigan, Dike was in Memorial Stadium, and when he saw some trackmen working out, he decided to join them.

"It was cold and raining, and the ground was muddy. Ray Eliot had just sent the gridders through a light workout, and Dike was in his football uniform, from heavy shoes to helmet. Herb Matter, a fine field event man, was high jumping, and Dike decided to join him.

"Herb had been working out in a light sweat suit, and had quit after clearing 5 feet 10 inches. But Dike, football uniform and all, cleared 6 feet 1 inch.

"Matter was so impressed that he called to tell me what had happened. 'That's about the greatest thing I ever saw,' Herb enthused. 'I don't know if there's another jumper in the country who could do that? The ground was soggy, so he couldn't get much spring, and those cleated football shoes are terribly heavy. To bring them over 6-1 without tipping the bar is marvelous. What a guy!'" said Shalit.

Back in the hunt for the championship title, the Illini beat Michigan 13-9 in Ann Arbor. This contest proved a delight for Illini Sam Zatkoff, a Michigan native who intercepted a Michigan pass. He ran it back 52 yards for the game-winning rally.

After the win vs. Michigan, the Illini received a scare from Iowa. Fortunately, it ended with a 7-0 win for Illinois. In the first half, it appeared the Illini had met their match. Three interceptions, by Ray Florek, Bernie Krueger and Dike Eddleman (Eddleman's being deep in his end zone), saved the day! By the

At age five, Dike played
outside from dawn to dusk.

While attending
Central Grade
School, Dike
excelled as a
basketball All-Star.
The All-Star teams
were comprised of
the best athletes
from Centralia's
seven grade
schools.

By eighth grade, Dike was beating the best high school jumpers.

As a Centralia High School freshman, Dike played on the varsity basketball team, scoring a record 24 points against Champaign in the 1939 state basketball tournament at Huff Gym.

Dike attended summer school at Culver Military Academy in Culver, Indiana, during his junior and senior years at CHS.

After Dike fouled out of the 1942 sectional tournament game, Farrell Robinson scored at the buzzer allowing Centralia to advance to the finals. Robinson and Eddleman bear Coach Trout's trademark, ankles taped like thoroughbreds.

Dr. William Lindenburg said, "All of us younger boys idolized Dike, and in his white shorts, football shoes and with sweat glistening on his bare arms and chest in the sun, he was the closest thing to a Greek god we had ever seen!"

Dike posed with Bill Nichols (right) after beating East Peoria at Centralia. Dike returned to football his senior year after suffering a knee injury during the first football game his freshman year.

Shy and unassuming, Dike was elected president of the student body at CHS in 1941.

Playing in the Illinois state basketball tournament three of Dike's four years in high school, the Orphans and Coach Trout won it all in 1942.

The 6'3" Eddleman easily high jumped over his girlfriend and future wife, the 5'1" Teddy Townsley.

At the end of his first semester of college, Dike was drafted into the Army Air corps in 1943.

Stationed in Miami Beach, Dike became a P.T. (i.e., physical trainer) for 20,000 new cadets.

While in the service, Dike and Ed Sadowski (right) played for the Wright Field Air Tecs and were recruited by Coach Charles "Chuck" Taylor (center) to play for the Converse All-Stars.

Coached by Northwestern's Arthur "Dutch" Lonborg, Dike played against the world champion Zollner Pistons as a 1945 College All-Star, wearing jersey number 3.

Teddy was Dike's number one
fan during his grade school,
high school, college and
military years.

Dike married his high
school sweetheart,
Teddy Georgia
Townsley, on
December 25, 1945,
at the First Christian
Church in Centralia.

Following Dike's discharge from the
Army in 1946, the newlyweds
returned to campus where Dike
enrolled in second semester classes.

An agile Eddleman carried the ball against Northwestern in front of a packed house at Memorial Stadium.

Excelling in football, basketball and track, Dike's favorite sport was basketball; his vertical jump put him head and shoulders above the rest in high school and college.

Dike perfected the "Kiss Shot," a shooting style described by sports writers as "more deadly than Clark Gable."

Dr. Harold Osborn, former Olympic gold medal winner in the high jump and the decathlon, was Dike's college mentor.

Teddy had Dike's favorite track shoes bronzed. Dike said they weren't his favorite pair; they were his only pair.

Dike qualified in the Olympic pre-trials at Northwestern's Dyche Stadium with a jump of 6'7¼" in 1948.

Following the 1948 Olympics, Dike and Teddy returned to a hero's welcome in Centralia which included guest speakers (at michrophone) Ray Eliot, Fred Wham, Leo Johnson, Harry Combes and Mayor H.B. "Shorty" Blanchard.

Dike's football photo made the cover of *Sport Life* magazine in 1948.

Meeting Bing Crosby and Bob Hope at Paramount Studios was a highlight of Teddy's trip to Pasadena.

Teddy flashed a victory smile at Dike when the couple returned to Champaign from the 1947 Rose Bowl.

Captain of the 1948-49 U. of I. basketball team, Dike carried the third-place trophy home from Seattle. Pictured from left to right: Wally Osterkorn, Dike, Jim Marks, Don Sunderlage, Dick Foley, Bill Erickson and Walt Kersulis.

When the Illini basketball team played in Seattle in 1989, members of the 1949 Final Four team gathered to reminisce. Pictured left to right: Jim Marks, Dike, Fred Green, former University of Illinois president Stan Ikenberry and Dick Foley.

Named Big Nine Conference MVP in 1949, Dike was awarded the *Chicago Tribune* Silver Basketball.

Dike played for the Tri-City Blackhawks, the Milwaukee Hawks, and the Ft. Wayne Zollner Pistons during his five years in the NBA.

After retiring from professional basketball, Dike returned to Illinois where he was employed as personnel manager for Central Soya, Inc. In 1956, Dike, holding his son Tom, posed for a family portrait with Nancy, Diana and Teddy. Kristy Ann, their youngest daughter, wasn't born until 1964.

Gregarious and fun-loving, the Eddlemans enjoyed giving and going to parties.

Joining John "Red" Pace (left) and Joe Skehen (center), Dike returned to his beloved University in 1969 to become executive director of the Grants-In-Aid (student-athlete scholarship program).

Cheering for the Chicago Cubs, Dike visited with WGN sportscasters Lou Boudreau (left) and Vince Lloyd (right).

Two Illini sport legends meet—Dike and All-America, All-Pro linebacker Dick Butkus.

Sharing Illini and Olympic memories are executive director of the U. of I. Alumni Association Lou Liay (left), Dike (center), and Olympic pole vaulter Rev. Bob Richards.

Louita Hartwell, Dike's loyal secretary, said, "If there were more men like Dike in the world, the world would be a much better place to live."

Former U. of I. basketball coach Lou Henson and Dike have traveled many miles together to attend Illini golf outings throughout the state.

U. of I. athletic director Ron Guenther is impressed with Dike's energy and enthusiasm.

When Dike retired, the University renamed its outstanding student-athlete award the Dike Eddleman Athlete of the Year Award.

Gov. Jim Edgar declared May 17, 1995 "Dike Eddleman Day" in Springfield. The proclamation was promoted by Senators Stan Weaver (left) and Frank Watson (right).

To Dike,
A great all-around athlete!!
Love,
Bonnie

Dike shares a smile with fellow Olympian Bonnie Blair.

Family members gather around Teddy and Dike in his trophy room.
From bottom left: Diana Lenzi, Kristy Eddleman, Tom Eddleman
and Nancy Hambright.

fourth quarter, Iowa was tired. Early in that period, Eddleman started the winning drive with a 15-yard punt return. Ruck Steger scored the winning touchdown.

Weather slowed the Illini against Ohio State. A fierce wind howled through Memorial Stadium as the Illini were forced to punt numerous times from their end zone. Buddy Young scored the first touchdown. Sam Zatkoff added a second-quarter safety. With the game hanging in the balance, Ohio State attempted a pass that was intercepted by Julie Rykovich on his 1-yard line. He raced 99 yards over a muddy field to score the winning touchdown in the Illini's 28-7 win.

Illinois shut out Northwestern 20-0 in the regular season finale. This was Illinois' first conference championship since 1928. Art Dufelmeier starred, gaining 123 yards in 10 attempts. That, in conjunction with Buddy Young's speed, Perry Moss and Bernie Krueger's quarterbacking expertise, and Dike Eddleman's greatest ground game of the season resulted in victory for the Illini, who also won a bid to the Rose Bowl!

The magnificent comeback of that 1946 football team created a memorable finish to the season. After being beaten by Notre Dame and Indiana, the road to the Western Conference Championship was a rocky one for the Illini.

Illinois' 8-2 record set the tone for loud and bitter denunciations from the nation's fans as the Fighting Illini prepared to play UCLA in the Rose Bowl on January 1, 1947. Undefeated UCLA said it was ill-matched with Illinois and wanted, instead, to play Army. That Rose Bowl game has become one of Illinois' favorite football stories. With the coaching skills of Ray Eliot and the student leadership of captain Mac Wenskunas, Illinois emerged victorious with a lopsided 45-14 win.

Illini teammates, wives and fans traveled to the Rose Bowl by train. Dike did not travel with the team to the Rose Bowl because the basketball team was scheduled to play the University of California at Berkeley on Friday and Saturday. (The Illini basketball team won Friday 58-36 but lost Saturday 53-35.) A conflict arose. Would Dike stay with the basketball team? Doug Mills and Ray Eliot decided that Dike would head to Pasadena and play in the Rose Bowl on New Year's Day.

Once in sunny California, the Illini were subjected daily to adverse headlines and sports reports. Bill Huber said, "I think that really worked in our favor. Every morning Ray Eliot would read these articles to us, and we would vow to show them we deserved to be at the Rose Bowl. Another terrific incentive for all of us was the promise of a gold watch if we won. Some of our players didn't even own a watch. And, much like the bowl rings of today, we all wanted to win one of those watches!"

One of Teddy's highlights was experiencing the glitz of Hollywood. The team was given a tour of Paramount Studios to see one of the legendary "Road" pictures, *Road to Morocco,* being filmed. During this tour,Teddy met Bob Hope and Bing Crosby. She has a picture of the three of them displayed in Dike's trophy room. During one of Hope's visits to the Assembly Hall, he autographed the picture for her. After that fabulous Western trip, which included a resounding victory, the Fighting Illini boarded the train to return home. For Dike, there was no rest because basketball season was under way.

Although Eddleman had fallen out of grace with basketball Coach Doug Mills because of the Rose Bowl, Dike enthusiastically rejoined Mills and his cagers because he loved basketball more than any other sport.

Switching from football to basketball was not easy. Eddleman said playing both sports continually was difficult because he used his legs differently. Yet, Dike never complained; he just trained harder. Even Coach Mills agreed. "Dike probably works too hard. If he has a fault, I'd say it's that he's too serious. He wants to excel at everything and always works to that end," Mills said in an article in the *News-Gazette* on January 7, 1947.

Illinois went 14-6 during the 1946-47 basketball season. Tying Indiana for second place in the conference, each finished 8-4. The former Whiz Kids, playing their senior year at Illinois, were less successful than before. The "Whiz Kids," an outstand-ing group of athletes originally comprised of Jack Smiley, Andy Phillip, Gene Vance, Ken Menke and Art Mathiesen, found Fred Green replacing Mathiesen, who had graduated. Playing back-up for the "Whiz Kids" were Dike, Bill Erickson, Walt Kirk, Jack Burmaster, Dick Foley and Bob LaVoy. Great expectations for an undefeated season prompted negative reviews. Doug Mills stepped down as head basketball coach after the 1946-47 season. He had promised the Whiz Kids he would coach them the year they returned from the service. Mills kept his promise.

1947-48

In 1947, as the defending conference champion, the Illini football team finished in a third-place tie at 5-3-1 after an up-and-down season. Upset losses to Northwestern and Purdue ruined what should have been an excellent season.

The Illini faced Pittsburgh in the season opener. Fans looked on in disbelief as 10 Illini lettermen played a mediocre game for three quarters. Playing in the backfield were Art Dufelmeier, Perry Moss, Paul Patterson, Ruck Steger and Dike. Sam Zatkoff, Bob Prymuski, Lou Agase, "Jocko" Wrenn, Herb Siegert, Bob Cruz and Ike Owens were the defensive line. Lou Levanti, a 200-pound center, was the only new player in Eliot's lineup.

The Pitt opener turned out to be a boon for Eddleman's football career because Dike clinched a starting position after producing the only two scores. After an interception by Art Dufelmeier on Pittsburgh's 46-yard line, Burt Schmidt got the foot-ball down to the 24. Perry Moss then whipped a short pass to Eddleman, who scampered between several defenders for six points. Minutes later, the Illini lost the ball on downs at the Pitt 3-yard line. Dike caught the resulting punt at the Pitt 42 and ran it back for another touchdown! The results: a 14-0 victory for Illi-nois and a guaranteed starting position for Eddleman at halfback. What a way to start a season!

The 35-12 rout against Iowa was memorable. Perry Moss' passing was spectacular, and Sam Zatkoff blocked punts all day long! Ruck Steger scored first and Eddleman added a touchdown to make it 14-0 after the first quarter. An amazing play occurred in the third quarter in which the Illini advanced 112 yards to score. Illinois had advanced 40 yards when Dike fumbled on the Iowa 24. An Iowa guard caught the ball in midair and started for the goal line. As he reached Illinois' 29-yard line, Art Dufelmeier hit him from behind, causing the Hawkeye to fumble the football to Ruck Steger, who finally scored on a 33-yard screen pass. This made the play a 112-yard advance. Chick Maggioli scored the final six points, sending the Hawkeyes home with a loss.

The Illini had a chance to end Army's 30-game winning streak in Yankee Stadium. This, compounded by all the publicity about who should have played in the 1947 Rose Bowl, set the stage for a spectacle. The Illini gambled at every opportunity, but Army refused to relent. The Illini completed 10 of 20 passes. Army played it safe, passing only four times with no completions. Although the game ended 0-0, the consensus was the Illini appeared the undisputed winners, leading in yards gained and in first downs.

Any fan who followed the Golden Era of University of Illinois sports remembers the 1947 gridiron battle with Minnesota. About 56,000 fans watched the greatest game of the season, a 40-13 Illini victory. Perry Moss, who completed seven passes in the first quarter, accounted for the first two touchdowns. Moss pegged a screen pass to Eddleman, who stepped over the goal line for six. Moss later tossed a 35-yard pass to Art Dufelmeier for the second touchdown. In the second quarter, Dike executed one of the season's most deceptive plays. Catching a punt on his 11-yard line, Eddleman crisscrossed the field, passing in front of Dufelmeier. The attention of the fans, the Illini blockers and the Minnesota tacklers was on Dufelmeier, who cleverly concealed the fact that Eddleman was romping 88 yards down the field for the Illini's third touchdown. With Illinois leading 20-7 at halftime, Minnesota got mad and marched 77 yards for a TD. The Illini retaliated with drives of 82 and 83 yards, the latter driven in by Dufelmeier for the fifth touchdown. Paul Patterson carried the next one in just before the gun sounded to end the Gophers' misery.

In the next game, Purdue took advantage of its underrated status and upset the Illini 14-7. Twelve minutes into the first quarter, Purdue scored, putting Illinois behind for the first time that season. In the second quarter, Perry Moss let loose with a beautiful spiral that Chick Maggioli took across the goal line. Purdue scored again in the third quarter, which found Eddleman kicking the Illini out of danger again. The Illini, failing to click in the fourth quarter, left West Lafayette with a loss.

Michigan, with a Rose Bowl bid and a Big Nine championship in the offing, showed no mercy vs. Coach Eliot's boys. Before 71,119 homecoming fans in Memorial Stadium, Michigan flexed the muscles that later would earn it a 49-0 Rose Bowl victory on January 1. Bump Elliott and All-American Bob Chappius racked up the Wolverines' points in a 14-7 victory. Ruck Steger smashed through a tackle and gained 53 yards for Illinois' only score.

Western Michigan's contest proved to be an exercise in conditioning as the Illini romped 60-14. Despite frigid weather, Coach Ray Eliot kept his team warm by using 38 players to roll up what was the third-highest score in Illinois history. Art Dufelmeier raced into the end zone on a 60-yard run 55 seconds into the contest. The second TD came on a 61-yard carry by Eddleman. Minutes later, Dike turned in the longest offensive play of the day, galloping 92 yards down the sideline on a punt return for an Illinois record he still holds. The result: 20-0 at the end of one quarter. During the second quarter, Western Michigan narrowed its deficit to 27-7. Denny Bassett gave reason for the half-frozen fans to go home as he scored early in the fourth quarter. Eddie Bray, a 1942 Illini great, then scored for a 54-7 lead.

Jack Pierce, also an Illini track man, finished the game with a 70-yard run to make it 60-14. On that chilly November Saturday, no one realized the significance of that 92-yard play by Eddleman, which remains the longest punt return in Illinois history five decades later. Dike actually broke his own record, which he set three weeks earlier with his 89-yard return against Minnesota. One year later, on the same weekend, Eddleman would set another school gridiron record with an 88-yard punt against Iowa.

Before a rain-soaked Ohio State crowd of 70,000, Illinois ruined Ohio State's homecoming with a 28-7 win. The Buckeyes held their own until the Illini scored in the second quarter. The second touchdown was a gutsy play from the 4-yard line. Dan Maechtle, Illinois' extra-point specialist, was sent into the game with everyone anticipating a field goal attempt. Much to Ohio State's surprise, Tom Gallagher jumped into the air and tossed a perfect pass to Chick Maggioli for an Illini TD. After a scoreless third quarter, the Buckeyes marched 59 yards to the 1-foot line! Running out of downs, Ohio State punted to the Illini 40. Perry Moss found Chick Maggioli in the end zone. With only two minutes remaining, Sam Zatkoff intercepted, and Paul Patterson scored the final points.

Northwestern handed the Illini a crucial defeat in the 1947 season finale. The Wildcats hissed their way out of the Big Nine cellar and bumped Illinois from its second-place conference position 28-13. A Dad's Day crowd watched bewilderedly as a championship-caliber Illinois team fell to a determined group of Wildcats. As Perry Moss' passes fell incomplete, Eddleman's punting kept the Illini out of trouble. Ruck Steger marched the ball 63 yards to the 2-yard line and dove across to score on the next play. Northwestern answered in the opening minutes of the second quarter for a 7-6 lead. A drive, led by Paul Patterson and Chick Maggioli, resulted in a 25-yard touchdown run. Don Maechtle kicked his 24th extra point of the season for a 13-7 lead. A Perry Moss pass intended for Paul Patterson was intercepted by a Wildcat, who cashed it in for a 14-13 halftime lead. A series of fumbles and broken plays turned into a fourth-quarter debacle for the Illini.

During the 1947-48 season, Dike led the Illini in scoring with 47 points. He became one of the greatest punters in college football history and was credited with the season's two longest touchdown runs.

Eddleman attributed much of his college football success to Coach Ray Eliot. "His speeches were spellbinding and inspired many of his teams to upset the giants of the conference. Over the years, he won many new friends for the university and re-kindled the loyalty of many alumni," Dike said.

The coach's locker room chats were awesome. Eliot's locker room speeches were fiery ones. They would send the teams charging onto the field, sometimes tearing the locker room door off its hinges. "I remember when we were playing Michigan, and the score was tied 7-7 at halftime," Dike said. "Ray was trying to get us up for the second half. After his talk, he took off his glasses, wiped his eyes and slowly said, 'My mother has her ear to the radio in New York, listening to the game and hoping that just by listening, she could help my boys win.' Well, we won 14-7, but I found out later that the game wasn't even broadcast in New York!" Eddleman said Eliot, besides being an outstanding coach, was a friend and companion to his players. He often would help them find jobs after graduation.

Eddleman and Eliot have many things in common, especially their allegiance to Illinois. "Illinois," Eddleman said, "was Ray's life." As a frequent spokesman for the university, Eliot wore his loyalty proudly but modestly. Eddleman recalled when a set of Illini blazers was being made up for Ray, he conspired with John Watkins, then owner of Delbert's Clothing Store in Arthur, Illinois, to sew a 'Mr.' in front of the 'Illini' on Eliot's blazers. "When Ray saw them, he insisted the 'Mr.' be taken off; Ray explained that 'there's a lot of Illini, and I'm one of them, the same as you are.'" "But he was Mr. Illini to me," Eddleman said. "There's no doubt about it."

The 1947-48 basketball season hit great heights as the team, under new Coach Harry Combes, tied for third place in the conference. Combes had replaced Mills, who became athletic director. Combes brought a faster pace to Illinois' game. The Illini led the conference in shot attempts and points scored. Illinois also used its depth as Combes regularly rotated starting lineups. Among the regular starters was Dike, now a junior. Coach Combes' style was more suited to Eddleman's ability.

Combes was calm and confident during his coaching debut at his alma mater. It was the players, perhaps trying to impress their new leader, who were nervous. Passing wildly and fouling needlessly, the Illini managed a 67-27 win over Coe College. By the second contest, the Illini had their game under control. Notre Dame, hailed as the preseason national champion, lost 40-30.

During Christmastime, the Illini traveled to Pittsburgh and Pennsylvania. Illinois won 70-33 and 70-44. Building on an eight-game winning streak, the Illini next played Washington State, which lost 71-35 and 59-42 in January 1948.

Traveling through a snowstorm and arriving two hours late for the tip-off, Harvard fell to the host Illini 77-41. Afterward, the Illini prepared for 11 consecutive conference games.

Wisconsin handed Illinois its first conference loss, 52-47 in Madison. The Illini rebounded vs. Northwestern. Captain Jack Burmaster contributed strong defense and scored 14 points in the 52-47 win. Against Ohio State, center Wally Osterkorn scored 17 points in a 61-58 victory.

One week later, the Illini did everything but stand on each other's shoulders to stop 6-10 center Jim McIntyre, who scored a sizzling 27 points in Minnesota's 59-51 victory.

Dike said there were some battles royal in the Big Nine that season. Perhaps none was as thrilling as the Illinois-Indiana contest in Huff Gym. Trailing 41-30 with seven minutes left, the Illini rallied as Van Anderson hit a buzzer beater for a 46-45 victory.

In a revenge match with Wisconsin, the Illini, paced by Dike's 16 points, emerged with a 57-36 victory. The hottest team Illinois faced in conference competition was Michigan, which taught the Illini a lesson in a 66-57 victory. Although the Illini lost, Eddleman scored 26 points with his famous "Kiss Shot." The Wolverines went on to win the conference title.

Dike tallied 26 points in the next game against Iowa, but Iowa's Murray Weir scored 36 points in the Hawkeyes' 70-61 win.

Coach Combes' men returned to Huff Gym for a spectacular scoring display against Purdue. The Illini set a single-game scoring mark in their 98-54 victory. Few doubt that the Illini's .553 shooting percentage in the second half could have been topped by any team that night!

After a routine 60-43 victory at Northwestern, the Illini capped the regular season with a 52-51 win at Indiana. Dike scored 20 points in the barn burner. Bill Erickson added nine points, and Fred Green had some frequent tip-ins. The die-hard Hoosier fans gave Dike the ultimate compliment during the game. In the heat of the contest while leaping for a rebound, Dike got more than the ball. He also got an elbow in the face—a blow so severe that it broke his nose! Coach Harry Combes removed Eddleman from the lineup, a measure that pleased neither the coach nor his players because Dike was hot that night. After receiving first aid, Eddleman sat on the bench next to Combes. Almost immediately, the Hoosier fans began yelling, "We want Eddleman! We want Eddleman!" Ignoring the chants, Combes subjected himself to a vigorous round of boos. With that, Eddleman got the nod from Combes to re-enter the game. The next day in the Bloomington newspaper, a reporter recounted the incident. One fan replied, "Hoosiers love to win, but they love a great basketball player even more!"

After returning from Indiana, Dike headed for class on Monday morning. While visiting with Doc Elhardt, his anatomy professor, Doc said Dike's nose looked crooked and he should have it checked. Sure enough, it was broken. The examining physician said it had to be rebroken and set. Dike was lucky because that was the only serious injury he received during his Illini basketball career.

Illinois finished 15-5 overall. The Illini finished in a three-way conference tie for third at 7-5. Eddleman led the team with 277 points. With only two seniors graduating, Jack Burmaster and Stan Fronczak, Coach Harry Combes and captain-elect Eddleman looked forward to a conference championship in 1948-49.

The 1947-48 Illini track team, under Leo Johnson's guidance, continued to dominate nationally. The Illini added to their laurels American and world records, an indoor and outdoor Big Nine championship, and an overwhelming victory in NCAA competition.

The team's strength was found in many talented individuals: Herb McKenley, Bob Rehberg, Bob Richards, Bill Mathis, John Twomey, George Walker, Norm Wasser, and, of course, Dike. This group formed one of the most powerful track teams ever seen!

In the season's first meet, a dual with Minnesota, the Illini broke 11 records in a 74-30 victory. To watch the astounding Herb McKenley run was to see poetry in motion. Eddleman recalled the Central Amateur Athletic Union Meet in which McKenley set a world record of 30.3 seconds in the 300-yard run. "I think Herb ran so fast during that meet because he was letting off steam. Before the race, someone had stolen his custom-made alligator shoes!" Dike said.

Led by the championship performances of Dike, Bob Richards, Bob Rehberg, Herb McKenley and George Walker, the Illini tallied the second-highest point total in conference history to win the Big Nine indoor and outdoor championships. 1947-48 was the best indoor track season for any Illini team since Leo Johnson took over in 1935. That season, Eddleman raised the Illinois high jump record to 6-7 1/4 for a Big Nine record and the championship.

Eddleman recalled an outdoor meet in Southern California. "It was hotter than 'blue blazes' — maybe 100 degrees on the day of our meet. We weren't used to that kind of weather, so we struggled to a 73-49 loss. That was our first dual meet loss in two years." The Illini managed first-place performances by Eddleman, Herb McKenley, Ron Leuthold, Bob Richards and Bob Rehberg.

Once again, Illinois continued to rout its Big Nine rivals at the outdoor championships. With McKenley winning two events and Mathis, Twomey, Eddleman, Richards and the mile relay team winning their events, the Illini accumulated 69 1/2 points.

At the NCAA meet, Herb McKenley ran his last races for the Orange and Blue, leading his teammates in a sweep. The 1947 Illinois track team was a dynasty! Eddleman contributed his share of points throughout the season, winning 24 major high jump titles.

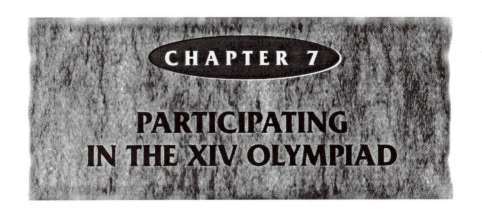

CHAPTER 7

PARTICIPATING IN THE XIV OLYMPIAD

During the summer of 1948, Eddleman traveled the road to athletic excellence that led to London, site of the XIV Olympiad. After years of practice and training, Dike earned an honor that many athletes never attain. July 10, 1948, proved to be a milestone in Eddleman's career. That day, he and teammate Bob Richards participated in the Olympic pretrial competition in Dyche Stadium at Northwestern University. Much to their surprise, they qualified for the London Olympics, Eddleman in the high jump and Richards in the pole vault.

The United States Track and Field Team was well-represented at the Olympic Games by a host of NCAA and Amateur Athletic Union athletes. Eddleman traveled to London with U.S. Track and Field teammates Herb McKenley, Harrison Dillard, Bob Richards, Clyde Scott and Bill Porter. Close friendships which were formed with his Olympic roommates, Clyde "Smackover" Scott from the University of Arkansas and Bill Porter from Northwestern University, have been maintained throughout the years.

After Eddleman and Richards qualified in their events at Northwestern, the Illinois athletes made a quick trip to Champaign-Urbana, leaving the next day to join the other American Olympic hopefuls in New York. Seely Johnston, owner of Johnston's Sporting Goods in Champaign and a noted sports historian, recalled returning to his store with the two athletes: "I gave them a leather valise, a pair of pants and a shirt. Neither of them had a suitcase, and they had to leave the next morning for London. I watched them both as they qualified at Dyche Stadium. I couldn't have felt prouder. They were two of the finest young athletes I had ever seen. More important than being talented athletes, they were fine young men." With leather bags in hand, Eddleman and Richards boarded the Illinois Central train that carried them to their Eastern destination.

The athletes were excited as they gathered in New York City. Many other athletes also had qualified only two or three days before leaving for London. High school and college students, grandfathers, housewives, filling station attendants, doctors, lawyers and preachers—they all came together with a common goal: to win the gold!

P. T. Barnum could not have created a more colorful scene than that aboard the *S.S.America*, the ship that carried them to the Olympic site. Regular passengers received a real show as the champions trained everywhere on the ship. "The oarsmen rowed across to England on special equipment nailed to the deck. The swimmers practiced in rope harnesses in the tiny swimming pool. The weight lifters snatched, cleaned and pressed 300 pounds on the sun deck. The runners streaked by on the promenade deck; the boxers danced on the sports deck; the riflemen shot targets from the ship aft," said Sandy Whitley, a nurse who traveled with the United States contingent.

Two doctors and two nurses held sick call twice a day. Sore throats, infected eyes, muscle strains and missing fillings were common complaints. No one wanted to take the chance of being physically handicapped to the smallest degree. The difference between winning and losing might be a blister on a foot or a cramped muscle.

Eddleman and the other Olympians were issued their uniforms and equipment on the ship. The United States teams looked dashing at the opening ceremonies in their Jon Wanamaker navy blue blazers with a red, white and blue insignia on the front pocket. The athletes also wore white slacks or skirts and white Panama hats. Eddleman said some female athletes had four-leaf clovers sewn under the Olympic emblems on their blazers.

Bob Kurland, one of the U.S. basketball players, was 7 feet tall. "The pair of slacks they gave him on the ship struck him just below the knees. A special uniform, large enough to fit him, had to be flown over to London. It arrived just in time for him to march in the parade of athletes," Dike said.

One of the trip's highlights was a variety show, staged two nights before the ship's docking, in which many athletes performed. It was a special night because curfew was extended from 10:30 p.m. until midnight. Eddleman did not perform in the show because he claims he was not blessed with the talent to sing or dance. He said confinement aboard the ship gave this group of Olympic contenders a special chance to socialize and develop new friendships. In no way were the athletes hampered by this mode of transportation. "All the athletes I knew felt well-rested and anxious to compete by the time we docked," Dike said.

After arriving in London, the red carpet was rolled out, and a gracious welcome was extended to everyone. England, and the rest of the world, welcomed an excuse to put aside the problems of austerity, ration books and thoughts about World War II, which had ended three years earlier. It was 12 years since the 1936 Olympic Games were held in Berlin. Following a precedent set after World War I, the World War II Axis powers, Germany and Japan, were not invited to compete in 1948. Communist countries were allowed to participate for the first time. Along with this came the first defections of Olympic participants.

Eddleman said there were mild complaints. "There was some dissension among the American sprinters, who complained that their coach had spent more time training Mel Patton, one of his own University of Southern California standouts, than he had Barney Ewell and Harrison Dillard. These were unfair accusations probably caused by anxiety," Eddleman said.

Arriving at their living quarters in London, some American teams found crowded practice areas or no practice sites. "I remember Coach Robert Kiphuth's swimmers and divers complaining about crowded conditions at the Wembley Pool. They could scarcely practice without kicking someone," Dike said. "I also remember our basketball team returning from an exhibition tour of Scotland and finding out they wouldn't even have a chance to practice on the Olympic floor at Harringay Arena before their game."

Under the circumstances, England did a magnificent job hosting the Games. About two million people attended the 16-day event. Of those, about 1.5 million paid admission fees of either $8 for a shady, dry reserved seat or 70 cents for standing room only.

Eddleman said the opening ceremony and the parade of teams were unforgettable. "It was my Olympic experience that made me realize that life is one continuous competition. Some days, you're a winner and on top of the world. Other days, you just have to muster up all your strength and courage and keep going," Dike said. "As Americans, we like to think we are smarter, live more comfortably, eat better and perform better than anyone else. To win events in the Olympics reinforces this sense of patriotic pride. After winning World War II, the U.S. was greatly admired and respected by the rest of the world. Being involved in that opening ceremony in London, I felt a sense of national pride that has never been duplicated."

The United States team entered Empire Stadium as the 56th of 59 teams. As the Games' 6,000 athletes walked through the tunnel into Empire Stadium at Wembley, 80,000 people clapped and cheered exuberantly. "The release of white pigeons, the presence of the Royal Family, the rousing music and all the color were overwhelming. It filled all of us with an unbelievable sense of pride. I will always remember the exhilarating feeling as we walked past the King and Queen of England. Representing the United States provided each and every athlete with a tremendous thrill!" Dike said.

That summer, the London weather was hot and humid with temperatures ranging from 80 to 90 degrees. Rain was a factor for many track and field contenders. Bob Richards said, "Dike and I were both plagued with the same problem. It rained on the day of our events. I really believe the weather had a bearing on our performances."

Newspapers said it was one of the hottest Olympics on record. Spectators collapsed and were carried out of the stadium approximately one per minute during the opening ceremonies. The first day, athletes stood and marched long hours under a blazing sun. Dike said the United States' 100-yard dash runners were excused from participating in the parade of athletes because of the extreme temperatures and lack of water. He also said several Boy Scouts, who carried banners for the nations, fainted and had to be revived in the infield.

"The opening ceremony itself only lasted about 10 minutes," Eddleman said. "Following the king's proclamation, 7,000 pigeons were released as symbols of peace. Then, there was a 21-gun salute from canons just outside the stadium, followed by the traditional lighting of the Olympic flame. It sent chills up my spine when the band played and a choir of 12,000 voices sang Handel's *Hallelujah* chorus." The athletes who had stood in ranks by country on the grassy infield then paraded back out of the stadium to their respective accommodations.

While in London, the U.S. Olympic Track and Field Team was housed at the Royal Air Force Base in Uxbridge, where athletes worked out on a track near their living quarters. The athletes had to be bused from Uxbridge to Wembley. Because of food rationing, box lunches were made for the Americans at Uxbridge and taken to the stadium each day. Eddleman vividly recalled accusations that the U.S. team had an advantage because it was better fed. "Food was scarce and extremely expensive in Europe after the war. Knowing this, the U.S. Olympic Committee brought food over on the ship for us. Food was never wasted. I remember some of the American athletes trading food items from their lunches for souvenirs such as pins or small flags," Dike said. "Basically, I think these accusations were created more for effect than from fact. One thing I do remember is that warm beer was easier to find than good drinking water."

Eddleman competed on the first day. After King George VI proclaimed the Games officially open, Eddleman's moment of truth arrived on July 30, 1948, when he had a chance to win a medal in the high jump.

John Winter, a 23-year-old bank clerk from Perth, Australia, injured his back after clearing 6-4 3/4. He tried one more jump anyway and made 6-6. Then, Winter watched in amazement as the remaining four jumpers, including two Americans who had cleared 6-7 1/4 just to make the American Olympic team, failed three times each. For the first time in Olympic history, ties were decided according to fewer misses.

The winning height was 6-6. The second-, third-, and fourth-place jumpers all cleared 6-4 3/4. Eddleman, who tied for second place, eventually was awarded fourth place because of his number of attempts.

Some controversy surrounded Eddleman's results. The official account of the running high jump, as it appears in the *Report of The United States Olympic Committee: 1948,* reads:

> This event was won by John Winter of Australia, who was the only man of the field able to clear 6'6". The three American entries were below their usual form. Verne McGrew, who won first place in the United States tryouts with a jump of 6" 8 1/2", qualified for the finals but did not place. George Stanich, who

tied McGrew in the tryouts and Dwight Eddleman, who jumped 6' 7 1/4" in the tryouts, were matched in height with Bjorn Paulsen of Norway and George Damitio of France at 6' 4 3/4". Because of the fewer jumps, Paulsen was awarded second place, Stanich was placed third, and Eddleman fourth. The International Amateur Athletic Federation jury later announced that these men would share second place but still later this decision was reversed.

Dike said, "George (Stanich) and I began jumping at 6 feet even. Paulsen started in at 6 feet, 2 inches. All three of us got up to 6-4 3/4. Then we tried for 6 feet, 6 inches. All of us missed except Winter from Australia. Winter had hurt his back during earlier competition but decided to make one final attempt. Able to clear 6 feet 6 inches, he was awarded first place with 6-4 3/4, the next highest jump."

"When the finals were over, the officials tried to decide who was second and who was third. They looked in the rule book but couldn't find an answer. We all had the same number of misses— three. So they went to Section A and found nothing. Then they looked in Section B. Still no help. Then they found something in the rule book about the guy who starts at the highest height having the advantage. George and I started jumping at 6 feet, and they counted it against us. Then later, they found out that the rule they used to clarify things only applied to first-place ties. Eventually, the three-way tie for second place was decided by the number of attempts actually made. This ruling was somewhat obscure in that the International Amateur Athletic Federation jury failed to ever give an explanation for all the reshuffling."

The reversed decision upset Dike. "Of course I was disappointed. They told us we had all tied for second place. Then, they changed their minds. Every game has rules, and you have to play by them. Whether you agree with the outcome or not isn't relevant."

Dike said none of the high jumpers performed up to par because they weren't allowed to practice with the standards and pit that were used in the finals. The standards were closer together than the athletes were accustomed, and the pit sand wasn't piled up. The pit was laid out angularly. "Without sounding like 'sour grapes,' these factors, plus the fact that we were kept waiting until late in the evening to complete the finals, threw most of us off stride," Eddleman said. "Incidentally, John Winter went 6-6 on only two occasions. One of those was at the Olympics."

Eddleman said he should have won first place at the Games. Teammate Bob Richards agreed. "Dike and I should have won our events. There's no question about it. What's really a shame is the fact that we didn't take the advice of Dr. Harold Osborn, a 1924 Olympian, who was the team physician at the University of Illinois. Dike got very little coaching advice while at Illinois. He was doing such a great job and winning all the time, so they were hesitant to change his style. But it was Dr. Harold Osborn who tried to convince us both to enter the decathlon. Dike was such a 'natural'; he could do it all. If Dike had been willing to try the pole vault, I really think he could have won the decathlon."

After an exhibition track and field meet in Glasgow, Scotland, where Eddleman won first place in the high jump at 6-6 1/2, he returned to the States with Bob Richards and other members of the United States Track Team aboard the *S.S. Queen Elizabeth*.

"Bob Richards was such a colorful guy," Dike said. "He bought a telephoto lens while he was over there. One morning, I woke up to find Bob at the top of a flagpole testing it out. My roommates and I got quite a laugh out of that. Obviously, his pole-vaulting had cured him of any fear of heights."

Eddleman recalled another amusing story concerning Richards' trip home after docking in New York. While in London, Richards, third-place medalist in the pole vault and, later, the first athlete to grace the front of a Wheaties box, had sold all of his belongings to purchase a British motorcycle. During the return cruise, Richards assembled the bike and, after docking, rode it all the way back to Champaign-Urbana!

During his return trip, Eddleman contemplated the words of Pierre de Coubertin, founder of the modern-day Olympics. "The important thing in the Olympic Games is not in winning but in taking part. The essential thing in life is not conquering but fighting well." After arriving in New York City, Eddleman was joined by Teddy. They flew back to Chicago after spending a few days in the Big Apple. After watching a Chicago Bears' football game, Teddy and Dike boarded the Illinois Central, which would take them to Centralia for a homecoming celebration.

Eddleman had represented his country with honor and returned home a hero. Merle Rogers, Dike's friend and schoolmate, shared his version of Dike's triumphant return to his hometown from the Olympic Games via the Illinois Central's "City of New Orleans." Despite the hot summer weather, Centralians turned out in droves to welcome their hero with banners, buntings, bands and guest speakers. The press and radio stations were positioned to cover the gala event. Rogers, a news reporter for radio station WCNT, wanted an exclusive interview—something special and personal with Eddleman's inner thoughts. This would be impossible among the thousands gathered for the reception and the parade.

Rogers got an idea to use the station's newest piece of portable equipment, a Sears and Roebuck table-model home recorder. Rogers quickly called the Illinois Central Railroad office to inquire if the train was equipped with 110-volt alternating current outlets. The answer was "yes" because electric shavers were used in the men's lounge.

Rogers improvised a wild scheme. He would have an associate drive him 60 miles north to Effingham, where he would board the train and record the interview in the lounge. Another staff member would meet him in Centralia; and while the remote broadcast crew covered the welcoming ceremonies, Rogers would return to the studio to play the personal interview on the air.

Rogers soon headed to Effingham to meet Eddleman's train. During the interview, Eddleman revealed—in his modest, humble manner—his deep appreciation for the loyalty and support of his friends and townspeople. Rogers recalled how the faint clickety-clack of train wheels punctuated the sincerity of Dike's remarks.

As the train screeched to a halt and the band struck up the rousing strains of Centralia's school song, the table-model recorder was spirited away for its three-mile trip to the radio station, where an engineer plugged it through the broadcast console, ready to air.

The reel was rewinding when the magnetic tape suddenly snapped and the machine spewed tangled filament all over the control room floor. Eddleman's gracious tribute to his fans lay there in a hopeless snarl of knots, never to be heard.

Although the recorded interview was lost, Eddleman thanked his many loyal supporters from the platform outside the Illinois Central Railroad station, where he was greeted by 3,000 cheering fans. He was presented with a sterling silver key to the city by Mayor H. B. "Shorty" Blanchard, who officially proclaimed Monday, August 23, 1948, as "Dike Eddleman Day." Standing on the platform with Eddleman were his former high school coach, Arthur Trout, and his University of Illinois coaches, Ray Eliot, Harry Combes and Leo Johnson. After being praised by his mentors, the Centralia sports hero was hoisted onto one of the city's fire trucks and paraded through the business district. This was the second public ovation extended to Eddleman. It brought back memories of the previous celebration in March 1942 when Eddleman and his teammates were honored as the state high school basketball champs.

Eddleman arrived in Centralia wearing his official Olympic uniform. In his white slacks, navy blue sports jacket bearing the United States Olympic insignia, a red-, white- and blue-striped tie, and his white Panama hat, Dike truly looked like everybody's "All-American." Dike looked tanned and handsome as he stood on the platform by his wife, Teddy, who was wearing a crisp, pale yellow dress and short white gloves.

After the speeches and ceremony at the Illinois Central station, Teddy was presented with a dozen long-stemmed red roses. Fred Wham Jr., the master of ceremonies, said after the parade Dike would attend the Rotary Club meeting for a luncheon in his honor. Before boarding the fire truck, Eddleman stepped into the crowd to greet family members. He was surrounded by a sea of pencils and paper from young and old seeking autographs.

His former coaches spoke at the Rotary luncheon, where more than 100 people honored him. The coaches were introduced by Chuck Flynn, then the University of Illinois' athletic publicity director. During his speech, Ray Eliot, Eddleman's college football coach, quipped: "I see your mayor has honored your boy, Dwight, with a key to the city. All of us up in Champaign thought Eddleman *was* the mayor down here." Eliot added he was "so darned proud of Teddy and Dike" he couldn't express it.

Coach Harry Combes, the U. of I. basketball coach, said it was difficult to remove Dike from a conference game even if he were injured. "Eddleman wants to get back in the game, the Illinois fans want him and the opposing fans scream for him. And there I sit," Combes said.

Leo Johnson, Dike's college track coach, described his athlete as a great "clutch" performer. He said the manner in which the Centralia star performed when the chips were down was legend in the Big Nine.

Before thanking the townspeople for the warm reception, Dike leaned over to Teddy and whispered, "I'd rather hit the Michigan line than talk." But once again, in the Eddleman style, he brought his audience to its feet. He expressed his gratitude for the homecoming celebration and for the nice comments the Illinois coaches had made about him. Turning to face them, Dike said he hoped to do better in all three sports next season.

After an 11-day respite, Eddleman found himself back onboard the Illinois Central. He was headed to Champaign-Urbana, where he would enroll for his final year at the University of Illinois. Less than two weeks after returning from London, he donned his shoulder pads and began practicing football in Memorial Stadium.

Eddleman called his trip to the Olympics a "real vacation." He finished his event on the first day of competition and had a couple of weeks to travel and sightsee. Teddy, who said Dike hates to shop, even found time to buy her a white silk blouse, a cashmere sweater and some crystal goblets.

"One thing that stands out in my mind about the whole experience is the fact that at the time, everybody in Europe was crazy about anything American. Somebody stole my Illinois track uniform, along with my leather football and my football cleats. I had taken them with me so that I could work out over there whenever I had a chance. I would have probably lost my rain jacket, too, but it rained so much over there, I wore it all the time," Dike joked. "I was lucky to get home with my uniform. A lot of guys had their whole uniform taken, while others found their buttons had been cut off. The gold buttons had the shield of the United States on them. Everyone wanted something from the U.S."

Eddleman regarded his Olympic medal as the greatest keepsake. "Prince Phillip presented us with our medals. We had to wait an hour to get them while he had tea," Dike said. "I remember he was tall and slender and a very likable guy. He really knew his track because he talked to us about the American records and best performances. Meeting him was truly a highlight of the trip."

Dike's Olympic homecoming celebration in Centralia was the work of several individuals. John Focht, an Alton newspaperman and a former Centralian, and two University of Illinois students, Bill Wilson and "Flip" Seely, masterminded the plan that shrewdly was orchestrated by Fred L. Wham Jr. Wham recruited Franklin Goodale, Ray Miller and W. H. Redaker to organize the affair. It was a special day for Teddy and Dike—a day they never will forget.

Receiving the key to the city of Centralia opened more than doors for Eddleman. It opened the hearts of all who knew him because, despite his accomplishments and honors, he remained modest, humble and unpretentious.

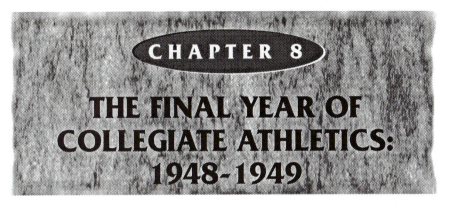

CHAPTER 8

THE FINAL YEAR OF COLLEGIATE ATHLETICS: 1948-1949

In August 1948, after a short visit to Dike's father's farm in Dongola, the Eddlemans returned to the University of Illinois.

Eddleman, the pride and joy of Centralia, now had become the pride and joy of Champaign-Urbana. Dike possessed the traits of a true champion: He was easy to coach, eager to learn and free of temper tantrums. In the Golden Age of Sports at the University of Illinois, Dike was the Golden Boy. During 1948-49, his list of athletic achievements lengthened.

In football, Dike set a new season punting record in the Big Nine, establishing himself as one of the greatest kickers in college with a 43-yard career average. He also contributed as a successful halfback on Coach Ray Eliot's football team.

Dike was captain-elect of the Illini basketball team that season and led the team with 329 points. He led his team to a Big Nine championship and, later, to third place in the NCAA Final Four in Seattle. To top off a sensational collegiate basketball career, Dike was named to Chuck Taylor's All-America Team. He also was awarded the Silver Basketball, presented by the *Chicago Tribune,* as the Most Valuable Player in the Western Conference after being selected as the Illini's MVP.

Touted as a second Jim Thorpe, the versatile Eddleman again won a multitude of collegiate high jump titles at the Illinois Tech Relays, the Central Collegiate Competition, the Kansas Relays, the Drake Relays and the *Chicago Daily News* Relays.

The 11 varsity letters Dike earned in football, basketball and track at the University of Illinois remains an unprecedented feat. Besides his many accomplishments in collegiate sports, Eddleman was named as Illinois' Athlete of the Year for the second time. He was awarded the jeweled pin from Sigma Chi fraternity for scholarship excellence. He also was inducted into Ma-Wan-Da and Atius-Sachem honorary fraternities. During the spring of 1949, Dike received the Conference Medal of Honor for his proficiency in athletics and academics.

FOOTBALL 1948-49

During Dike's senior year, the Illini football team had a better season than its 3-6 record would indicate. During that season, Dike said Eliot's players were small in stature but mighty in spirit. "The biggest thing our team had that season was our desire to win!" Eddleman said.

The 1948 season opener against Kansas State pleased Eddleman because the 40-0 final score included his "magic" jersey number. Illinois led only 7-0 at halftime. Scoring 33 points in the second half, the Illini generated excitement for the ecstatic fans who filled Memorial Stadium. With touchdowns from fullback Burt Schmidt, Paul Patterson and Jim Valek, the Illini were off to what appeared to be a great season.

In the conference opener against Wisconsin, the Illini surrendered a late lead and lost 20-16. Until the game's final minute, it appeared Illinois would win 16-14. On fourth and 5, the Badgers tried a field goal. As the ball sailed wide, the Illini began to celebrate. An offsides penalty, however, gave Wisconsin a first down on the Illini 7-yard line. Given another chance, the Badgers pushed across to score a TD. Dike's punting, which set up Illinois' touchdowns, was the highlight.

"Bad blood" still existed between Illinois and Army because of the Illini's 1947 Rose Bowl bid. Army's caissons came rolling into Memorial Stadium for the third game of the season. Army wasted no time in placing a 26-0 score on the board in front of 71,000 enthusiastic fans. In 17 minutes, though, Illinois fans became hysterical as the Illini trailed 26-21. The Fighting Illini rally began when Lyle Button recovered a fumble on Army's 26-yard line. Bernie Krueger passed to the two-yard line and then scored. Surprising Army, Jack Pierce returned a punt 65 yards to the 22, which set up a score by Paul Patterson. With some perfect passing by Krueger and some remarkable running by Sammy Piazza, Illinois tallied its third touchdown. Mustering up too little, too late, the Illini fell by five points.

Minnesota and Illinois were so evenly matched, it appeared the contest would end in a tie until two Gopher substitutes sparked a 76-yard scoring drive. The Gophers fumbled nine times, and the Illini lost the ball four times. Illinois threatened to score twice, but the Gophers won, 6-0.

Eddleman and his teammates played before a full house at Memorial Stadium on I-Men's Day and emerged with a hard-fought 10-6 win vs. Purdue. The Illini surprised the Boilermakers with a tough defense that held Purdue to 98 yards rushing. Don Maechtle made his first field goal of the season. Illinois tallied its final points after Purdue botched a punt that went to its 17-yard line.

The Ann Arbor homecoming game could have been named "The Battle of the Breaks." Unfortunately, the Illini were not on the receiving end and bowed to Michigan, 28-20. The Fighting Illini nearly pulled off one of their greatest upsets. The fight and determination of Coach Ray Eliot's boys drew the accolades of the national news service. Dike recalled the heartbreaking misfortunes suffered against the nation's top team. "Illinois played a heck of a game. After Michigan scored, Illinois went 72 yards for a TD," Dike said. "Tom Stewart threw me a 38-yard pass, and Paul Patterson made a 10-yard run off a screen pass to score." It was on the second-half kickoff that Lady Luck turned her back on the Illini. Dike recalled, "Just before the referee whistled for the second-half kickoff, Jack Pierce waved and ran over to me to clarify the next play. I received the kickoff and Jack and I ran a crisscross play. The Wolverines must have thought Jack was taking the handoff because he got buried. I kept the ball and ran 94 yards for what would have been the longest kickoff return ever made against a Michigan team. Even the Michigan crowd booed when the offsides call was made. The official had thrown his flag because Lyle Button stepped on the chalk line. Another bad break gave Michigan the ball on pass interference on the 1-yard line. They scored on the next down." Such tough breaks could have crushed the Illini morale. However, the fight in the Fighting Illini prevailed as Jim Valek recovered a fumble and Bernie Krueger completed 12 passes for 218 yards and a touchdown. Burt Schmidt and Slip Kersulis were on the receiving end of Krueger's passes to complete a 68-yard touchdown drive that brought the score to 21-20. With time running out, Michigan scored another TD for the win.

The Iowa game proved to be another one of Eddleman's great punting performances as he hit on two quick kicks, one for 74 yards and another for 88 yards. Murney Lazier's fabulous 56-yard punt return and Ruck Steger's 1-yard plunge gave Illinois a 14-0 victory over the Hawkeyes. Eddleman's 88-yard kick against Iowa on November 6, 1948, remains in the University of Illinois record book. "Lots of people ask me about the '48 Iowa game. It was a great day for me. Weather plays a big factor in football. Although it was November and a strong wind was blowing through Memorial Stadium, I recall having really good rhythm that day. My legs felt strong. I kicked several over the receivers' heads, and they rolled out of bounds just short of the goal line. That day I punted six times for 318 yards for a 53-yard single-game average."

More than 65,000 chilled fans witnessed the Illini's home-coming debacle against powerful Ohio State, which turned a 13-7 game into a 34-7 rout in the fourth quarter. For three quarters, the Illini held the Buckeyes to only two touchdowns. Toward the end of the third quarter, Slip Kersulis grabbed a Krueger pass out of the air and crossed the goal line for the Illini's only touchdown. As the fourth period started, the Buckeyes marched 76 yards to score. Their next two scores were giveaway plays set up by the Illini. A kickoff by Ohio State, after one of its touchdowns, hit Lou Levanti in the chest. Recovering on the Illini 44-yard line, the Buckeyes quickly scored. On another play, Ohio State's punter could not get his kick off because of the Illini's rush. He ducked and ran 55 yards down the sideline for another touchdown. Eddleman, who averaged 53 yards on six kicks, was one of the few bright spots.

Although the Illini lost their final game to Northwestern, Eddleman established a Big Nine season punting record by averaging 42 yards a kick. The Wildcats were crowned the Big Nine champions after their 20-7 victory. Despite the Illini loss to Northwestern on November 20, 1948, Dike contributed his best collegiate football performance ever, kicking 401 yards on nine attempts.

BASKETBALL 1948-49

Dike's senior basketball season proved more successful than his final football season. The Fighting Illini, under the leadership of No. 40, became the 1949 Western Conference champions and beat such highly rated teams as Butler, Notre Dame, Oklahoma and Minnesota. The team was nicknamed the "Forty-Niners" because of its never-say-die attitude. Not only did the players earn special honors, but Coach Harry Combes, in his second year at Illinois, also was named Coach of the Year. The team set conference and season scoring records. Illinois' "Forty-Niners" struck pay dirt regularly, finishing 21-4 overall and 10-2 in the conference.

During the season's first game against Butler, Walt "Ox" Osterkorn poured in 27 points to lead the Illini to a 67-62 win. Next, a highly rated Notre Dame team set the pace for the rest of the season. At the end of regulation, the score was tied at 56. Eddleman, driving for a basket, drew a foul for two free throws. Dike made only one, and Notre Dame responded with a quick basket. With only 15 seconds left, Bill Erickson spotted Burdette Thurlby alone beneath the basket. After a perfect pass, Thurlby netted the winning goal for a 59-58 Illini win.

Illinois stumbled against DePaul, losing 60-50. However, the shooting slump was short-lived as the Illini came back to beat one of the season's top teams, Oklahoma, 73-68. In a revenge match against DePaul, the Illini prevailed 89-51.

In December 1948, Eddleman gave Coach Harry Combes and his teammates an early Christmas present when he averaged more than 20 points a game against Indiana, Ohio State, DePaul, Cornell and Colgate.

The Western Conference opener was a relative breeze as Illinois beat Wisconsin 62-50. The starting five built a 60-32 lead, and the reserves held on.

Road games to Indiana and Ohio State were next. These last-minute thrillers proved to be the deciding factors in the conference race. It took the Illini two overtimes to edge Indiana 44-42. Although Indiana led 37-31 with less than five minutes to play, Don Sunderlage and Bill Erickson closed the gap for a 37-37 tie. The first two points in overtime came from a 40-foot "Kiss Shot" by Eddleman. When the first overtime ended 40-40, Coach Harry Combes placed the "long and tall" Fred Green into the lineup. With four seconds left on the clock in the second overtime, Green hit a high-arching shot for a 44-42 win!

In a down-to-the-wire thriller, the Illini scored in the final 16 seconds to edge Ohio State 64-63. Center "Ox" Osterkorn was the hero, scoring a basket and a free throw in the last seconds. High-scoring efforts by Osterkorn, Fred Green, Bill Erickson and Dike proved too much for the Buckeyes.

The next conference opponent was Big Nine leader Minnesota. With a 45-42 lead, Illinois started a "four corners" stall with more than 2 minutes left. The Gophers got possession only once in those final minutes, and the Illini won 54-44!

The Illini dropped their next game against Purdue. Van Anderson missed a 10-foot shot in the final seconds as the Illini fell 55-53.

Wisconsin had gained momentum since its first encounter with Illinois. The next meeting required a second-half comeback by the Illini. Illinois trailed 29-28 at halftime, but "Pirate" Thurlby tallied 11 points in seven minutes to put the Illini in front en route to a 61-54 win.

Eddleman and his teammates found their range against Northwestern, winning 85-66 and 81-64. Against Iowa, Eddleman connected for 19 points in an 80-49 victory.

The Fighting Illini set a record against Indiana, swishing 19 consecutive free throws. In the 91-68 win, the Illini scored 31 points from the charity stripe. Assured of the conference championship, the Illini fell to Michigan 70-53 to end an outstanding regular season. After the Michigan game on March 7, 1949, there was a two-week break before Illinois' first NCAA contest.

On Monday, March 21, 1949, Harry Combes' Western Conference champions traveled to Madison Square Garden in New York to play Yale in the opening game of the NCAA Eastern Regional tournament. The game was tied nine times before Illinois pulled out a 71-67 victory.

Yale's Tony Lavelli played an outstanding game. Most of Lavelli's 27 points came from an indefensible hook shot. He was also 7 for 7 at the free throw line.

In the early stages, Dike said both teams were nervous and missed simple shots. Dike provided the only spurt of excitement in the first half when he kissed in the first of five consecutive baskets.

Eddleman gave Dick Foley credit for Illinois' first-round win. "Dick came in with about three minutes left. We were behind 64-59. His passing game enabled us to finally play effectively against Yale's zone defense."

The Fighting Illini were thrilled to advance in the tournament. Next they faced Kentucky, the defending NCAA champion. Kentucky had defeated Villanova in the second game of the first-round doubleheader in the Garden.

On March 22, 1949, Illinois' victory celebration was cut short. Kentucky humbled Illinois 76-47. Kentucky advanced to play Oklahoma A & M in Seattle for the national title. Illinois traveled to Seattle for the third-place game against Oregon State, the Pacific Coast champs.

"All of us seniors—which included me, Jim Marks, Fred Green and Dick Foley—vowed to make a good showing in our final game for Illinois. Kentucky had dominated us, and we were determined to end our college careers on a winning note," Dike said.

The Illini defeated Oregon State 57-53 in a hard-fought game. "Ox" Osterkorn and Dike were high scorers with 17 and 11 points, respectively.

Dike said Oregon State played physically. "After the game, Coach Combes told reporters he wondered if he had brought along enough players when three of us—me, Green and Osterkorn—fouled out. I think Bill Erickson and Dick Foley had four fouls apiece. The great thing about that final game was we all stepped up to contribute and came home winners," Dike said.

After catching a United Airlines flight to Chicago, the team boarded the Panama Limited, which delivered it to the Illinois Central station in Champaign.

Eddleman, as team captain, made a short speech. Speaking from the steps of the train, Dike thanked the fans who had gathered to greet the team. As Dike held the third-place trophy, he beamed. "We certainly appreciate how you've been faithful to us, not only this time, but all season long. We had a great time in Washington. Everyone was pulling for Oregon, but the town was basketball crazy, and they went out of their way to treat us nicely."

Despite the bitter loss to Kentucky, the 1948-49 Fighting Illini basketball season went down in the record books as an accomplished one. Not only had the team earned the eighth conference title in Illinois' basketball history, but it also was the first Illinois team to compete in the NCAA tournament finals. Its 21-4 record was the third best in Illini basketball history. The team established Illinois and conference season scoring records, tallying 1,705 points in 25 games for a 68.2 average. In conference play, Combes' sharpshooters scored 783 points, which broke the previous mark of 755 points held by the 1943 Whiz Kids.

Eddleman established a season scoring record with 329 points, erasing Andy Phillips' 1943 record of 305. Scoring 606 points in his last two collegiate basketball seasons, Eddleman established a two-year scoring record at Illinois. In addition, he was elected the team's most valuable player.

His MVP status led to another accolade that was presented by the *Chicago Tribune*. Dike received the regulation-sized *Chicago Tribune* Silver Basketball Award on March 24, 1949, at a luncheon at the LaSalle Hotel hosted by the Illini Club of Chicago. The presentation was made by Wilfred Smith, a *Tribune* sports writer.

Eddleman was named by a committee of the nine conference coaches, nine game officials, Kenneth L. Wilson, the conference commissioner, Arch Ward, sports editor of the *Tribune,* and Wilfred Smith. The Illini captain was chosen by this committee from a group of nine nominees, each of whom had been chosen by his teammates as the MVP for their respective squads.

Dike became the award's fourth recipient. Others to have received it were Max Morris of Northwestern, Glen Selbo of Wisconsin and Murray Weir of Iowa. In the vote of the 21-member committee, Eddleman received 13 first-place ballots and two second-place ballots. The votes, worth two points and one point, respectively, gave Eddleman 28 votes, which doubled the number received by the second-place nominee, Dick Schnittker of Ohio State.

The week after his final basketball game for Illinois, Eddleman was honored as the "college football player of 1948 exerting the most wholesome influence on today's youth" by the Christian Athletes Foundation of Hendersonville, North Carolina. The announcement was made by the Rev. C. E. Jackson. Amos Alonzo Stagg, advisory coach for Susquehanna University in New York, and "Dad" Elliott, Northwestern University football great and an evangelist, also were honored by the foundation. This latest claim to fame caused Dike to become one of the hottest commodities on the local spring banquet circuit. He scheduled as many engagements as he could fit into his track schedule.

TRACK 1948-49

Having lost many first-place record holders, Coach Leo Johnson and his 1948-49 track squad proved their strength was their depth of talent. Snagging second in the Big Nine indoor meet and third in the Big Nine outdoor meet, the determined track men won all their dual meets. They also retained the Illinois Tech Relays trophy and the Central Collegiate crown.

In the season's first indoor meet, Baldwin-Wallace College brought its great star, Harrison Dillard, to compete in the Armory, where he tied two hurdles records. Dillard and Eddleman competed on the U.S. Track Team in the 1948 Olympics in London. One thing Eddleman liked about competing was making friends with athletes from around the country and the world.

After handing Baldwin-Wallace a 79-35 defeat, the Illini rolled over Michigan Normal, 77-36, and Indiana, 78-54. Ohio State edged Illinois by three points to win the conference's indoor meet.

Every athlete probably has a "what if" scenario. Besides wondering what Eddleman's point totals in basketball would have been *if* there had been three-pointers *and* besides wondering what his kicking stats would have been in football *if* he played by today's rules (in the 1940s, 20 yards was subtracted from the distance if the ball was kicked into the end zone), Leo Johnson had to wonder *what if* Eddleman had high-jumped in the Big Nine conference indoor meet in 1949? Dike didn't jump because he was playing in the Final Four.

Eddleman, had he jumped well, probably would have taken first place, moving his competitors down a notch. That would have increased the high jump point total from six to nine. This would have put Dike first, Lou Irons third and Harry Andersen tied for fourth. Ohio State's totals would have dropped from five points to four with John Murphy placing second instead of first. Then, Illinois would have tied Wisconsin for the Big Nine title with 38 points. Ohio State would have finished third with 37. Not only would Illinois have tied for the first-place conference title, but Dike also would have won his indoor high jump title for the fourth consecutive year. So although it seems Dike did it all, even he has his "what if" stories.

During the outdoor season, Eddleman again won his event at the Kansas Relays and the Drake Relays. Back-to-back meets with Minnesota and Purdue saw Illini victories of 72-60 and 78-54, respectively. Big track names for the Orange and Blue included Walt Karkow, Bill Buster, Paul Behan, Norm Wasser, Don Leuthold, Lou Irons and Paul Huston.

When his collegiate athletic career ended in spring 1949, Eddleman had a roomful of trophies, medals and gold watches. Eddleman's long and illustrious college career, extended by the war, came to an end with his graduation on June 12, 1949.

When the track letters were presented at the spring banquet, Dike Eddleman, the greatest all-around athlete in Illinois history, walked to the podium for the last time. As he accepted his 11th "I," there was no fanfare or special recognition—just a "congratulations, Dike," from Coach Leo Johnson and a "thanks, Leo," from Dike. Performing in a few more meets for Illinois, including the Big Nine-Pacific Coast (Pac 10) meet and the Texas AAU meet, Dike's college career came to a close.

In an attempt to immortalize Dike's stellar athletic career at the University of Illinois, an effort was made to retire his No. 40 jersey. An article written by Flip Seely for the *Centralia Sentinel* in July 1949 reported that George Ross and friends had amassed 12,000 signatures in support of this cause. The signatures included firsthand endorsements from Red Grange, Andy Phillip, Lowell Spurgeon, every member of the Illinois basketball, football and track squads, and several other prominent individuals. More than 250 high school coaches and three metropolitan newspaper editors voted approval of the retirement. The petitions were presented to the Athletic Association Board, which referred the matter to an Athletic Association "committee." The "committee" was given the petitions after the second semester in 1949, and it was to decide the matter at its next meeting in September. According to George Ross, the petitions were presented to Athletic Director Doug Mills, but the subject never was discussed.

CHAPTER 9

EDDLEMAN'S CAREER IN THE NBA

Appropriately, Thomas Dwight Eddleman re-ceived his college diploma in Memorial Stadium, the site of some of his greatest triumphs. It was there that Dike won three high jump championships as a Centralia high school boy. It was there that he set the Illinois outdoor record of 6 feet, 6 inches on a high jump pit he never really liked. It was there he ran 40 yards from scrimmage and 87 yards on a punt return to beat Pitts-burgh 14-0 in the 1947 football season opener. It was there where he set several kicking records, including most punts in a career (159), most yards punted (6,128.5), most yards punted in a sea-son (2,535), most yards punted in a game (401), longest punt (88) and best season average (43). The crowd roared as Eddleman stepped up to receive his diploma from George Stoddard, univer-sity president, during commencement.

For two weeks after graduation, Eddleman competed in track under the auspices of the University of Illinois in the Big Nine-Pacific Coast Meet at Berkeley and the National AAU Meet in Texas. After those meets, the time arrived for the many lettered, wrist watch-bedecked "Bad Man Eddleman" to carry his athletic name into the world of professional sports. After graduating with a bachelor's degree in physical education, Dike received numerous offers to pursue professional careers in three sports—football, basketball and baseball.

During their senior year at Illinois, Dike and Al Mastrangeli were chosen to play in Arch Ward's College Football All-Star game. Although Dike did not play in that game, he had proven successful as a college halfback and punter which brought professional football contract offers from the Cleveland Browns, the Chicago Bears and the Detroit Lions. Dike declined these offers because he thought his high school knee injury might limit his performance as a pro football player.

In the February 26, 1949, issue of the *Saturday Evening Post,* Jerry Thorp wrote a four-page spread about Eddleman's versatile sports career. Although Dike had played softball in an amateur league in Centralia, he never had spent much time playing baseball. He had, however, played baseball while attending Culver Military Academy during the summer of his junior and senior years in high school. When Thorp asked Eddleman about the prospects of a professional baseball career, Eddleman replied, "I didn't think much about baseball until I got offers from the Cubs, the Reds, the Cardinals and the Dodgers. I told them I didn't know much about baseball. They said that was all right, they'd teach me."

Eddleman thought he had the greatest chance at success playing basketball, his first love. His professional basketball career began after he received offers from the Chicago Stags and the Tri-City Blackhawks. He decided to play for the Blackhawks because he preferred to live in Moline, Illinois, with his wife and newborn daughter. The first of four children, Diana, was born in Champaign, Illinois, on July 2, 1949, just weeks after Dike's college graduation.

A picture of Diana and her proud parents was published with the headline "Cheerleader Born to Teddy and Dike." Although Dike wanted his first child to be a son, he wasn't disappointed. Teddy took Diana to watch Dike's pro games. "Diana got accustomed to staying up late and sleeping in. She loved watching her dad play basketball," Teddy said.

Dike enjoyed being a part of the fledgling National Basketball Association. "I signed my first contract with the Tri-City Blackhawks for a little over $8,000 per year, and my last one with the Zollner Pistons for around $30,000. That was a respectable amount in the 1950s."

Even now, when Dike travels to the Quad-Cities area, which includes East Moline, Moline, Rock Island and Davenport, he feels nostalgic as he nears the Short Hills Country Club. He remembers wonderful friends such as John Hobart, Al Hallene, Red Summers, Don Otten and Gene Vance. Playing professional basketball was a dream-come-true for him. Sports always has been his passion in life.

Gene Vance, a former Fighting Illini Whiz Kid who works as a consultant for the University of Illinois Foundation, referred to those early days as the "Dark Ages" of professional basketball. "Some of the leagues were located in small towns such as Sheboygan, Wisconsin. I remember many games were played in high school gyms. Those smaller arenas would pack in the fans. I remember one game in which spectators sat in folding chairs inches from the out-of-bounds lines. They sold peanuts-in-the-shell during the games. You'd really have to be careful because by the end of the game, you'd go sliding on the empty shells right into the audience!"

On November 10, 1949, the Blackhawks hired Arnold "Red" Auerbach as their head coach. Four days after Red was hired, the Blackhawks played in Moline's Wharton Field House, a gym constructed in the '30s with a capacity of 6,100. The Blackhawks beat the Waterloo Hawks 99-89 for Auerbach's first Tri-City victory. Eddleman enjoyed playing for Coach Auerbach, and the feelings were mutual. "Dike was a hard worker and an earnest competitor," Auerbach said.

On December 13, 1949, the *Chicago Daily News* sports page heralded the headline: "Eddleman Sure-Fire Hit With Tri-City Five."

An Auerbach quote from that same article described the rookie in those days. "He's an atom bomb of energy—ready to explode. Dike will be even better when I teach him how to relax."

An article printed in the *Rock Island Argus* in December 1949 reported, "Dike Eddleman, of Illinois fame, was never more brilliant, although his scoring of fifteen points was somewhat off his best showing. The all-sport star from Centralia was impressive as he zoomed all over the floor setting up baskets, rebounding and playing defense." Once again, Eddleman had aimed high and attained his goals. He had made it in the pros.

Red Auerbach continued through the fledgling NBA ranks and became the legendary coach of the Boston Celtics. Wharton Field House was one of the arenas where the NBA, in its infancy, was taking root. It was in Wharton Field House where Pop Gates, the first black pro, played basketball. Don Otten, the pro's first 7-footer, played there, too. Great things were happening in Moline's famed field house in the '50s, and they would have a profound effect on the future of professional basketball.

Fans were loyal. There were nearly 4,500 season ticket holders. During the 1949-50 season, Dike's first in the pros, the Blackhawks drew 155,478 fans for 35 home games. Bolstered by the addition of the former Illini Whiz Kid, the Tri-City team finished 29-35. That year, the Blackhawks were one of only four pro teams (out of 22) that made a profit.

The owners realized there was big money to be made and reacted accordingly. Blackhawk games usually were played at 8:30 on weeknights and 3 p.m. on Sundays. During Dike's first season, the team played 64 games. Sometimes, there were as many as five games scheduled a week.

It was great fun being a player in those days. "If we had only realized where this sport was going, we could have made millions," Dike said. He recalled hearing that at one of the league meetings in those days a franchise had been offered for sale for $500.

Even in its formative years, pro basketball drew crowds that loved to raise a ruckus. Fans felt much freer to pick on the pros rather than the local prep players. "The crowds used to get on big Don Otten a lot!" Dike said.

Referees were open targets, too. Dike recalled Bill Downs, a bald-headed official who also was the commissioner of O'Hare Airport. "He used to yell right back at people when they heckled him. One night, I remember him saying to someone in the audience, 'Let me borrow your comb so I can see the next call better.'" Dike also said referee Jim Enright ran straight for the dressing room—out of necessity—at the end of a game after bellowing his calls all night.

During his first NBA season, Eddleman averaged 12.9 points as the Blackhawks' leading scorer. He still was able to connect on his set shots with amazing accuracy. One Associated Press reporter described Dike's shooting as follows: "He arches the ball as high as possible and, as if radar-directed, it usually swishes the cords without hitting the rim or the backboard." In his second NBA season, he boosted his average to more than 14 points a game. After four seasons, he had scored 3,296 points, averaging 12.6 points a game. He was by no means a Michael Jordan. He was, however, one of the prominent pioneers of professional basketball.

With success comes pressure. So it was in the 1950s. Alcohol was no stranger to some of the pro players. Russ Kiesele, sports editor for Moline's newspaper *The Dispatch*, said, "There were some players who were real boozers. I'd see some of them show up for games half-bombed, and they'd go out and play a hell of a ballgame. They were good ballplayers. When they were half-bombed, they would play loose and relaxed, and everything they threw up would go in the basket."

Dike and Teddy frequented the Time-Out Bar on Sixth Avenue and 14th Street in Moline. It was owned by two Blackhawk players, Billy Hassett and Whitey Von Neida. A five-foot mural of the Blackhawk team hung on the wall. It was a popular place where everyone went after the games.

Teddy did her best to keep Dike's stress in check. Dike found the road games tiring. "Traveling sounds glamorous, but it was difficult," Dike said. Nearing 30, he began feeling the aches and pains that accompany pro sports. "Dike worried about staying healthy. Injury or poor performance might have ended his career," Teddy said.

Dike's first move in the pros was from Moline, Illinois, to Milwaukee. This change came when Fred Miller, owner of the Miller Brewing Co., acquired the team. Ben Kerner, who previously owned the Blackhawks, was told by the league that Wharton Field House was too small. Some fans hadn't even heard of the Tri-Cities. The Blackhawks weren't drawing large enough crowds at away games. Consequently, the team moved to Milwaukee and became known as the Hawks.

Dike and his family called Milwaukee home for the next year. Home turned out to be a hotel room. With a child, that lifestyle was far from ideal. Dike later was traded to the Fort Wayne Zollner Pistons. The trade was made on the night the Hawks played the Pistons. Dike was hot and scored a league-high 48 points.

As a Piston, Eddleman played in two consecutive NBA All-Star Games in 1951 and 1952. After Dike's trade to the Pistons and the move to Indiana, Dike and Teddy were happier. Fort Wayne was the first place they finally could call home. There they purchased their first house, a small bungalow just down the street from Charlie Share, the Zollner's big center.

Share recalled that era of professional basketball and Eddleman's unique style. "I can honestly say Dike was one of the most social, congenial and fun-loving ballplayers I can recall from that time. On the basketball court, I recall an accurate, but now obsolete, two-handed 'Kiss Shot.' Some called it a rainmaker because of its high arch. Dike could make that shot from almost any distance. His freewheeling spirit might have reflected itself on the court as there were those close to him who would suggest good-naturedly that he'd shoot from the locker room if the door was open! I do believe that was the first time I'd heard the expression, but have heard it many times since! Off the court, his social nature always exposed itself when I walked up the street, set foot in his house and responded affirmatively to his offer, 'Here, Charlie, have a beer!'" Team members socialized together. "There were enjoyable parties which all the team members attended at Dike and Teddy's house as well as ours. For the most part, our relationships in those days revolved around basketball games and our respective children."

Teddy and Dike began to feel more like a family in Fort Wayne. Their lives revolved around the Pistons games and the people who made up the Pistons world. Their friends included Marcie and Tom Sheets. Marcie worked for the Pistons' front man, Rodger Nelson, who Teddy described as a "man about town." He was the one who ran the organization. Carl Bennett was in charge, but Rodger always knew what was going on. He was a big help to the players. The Eddlemans still visit their Hoosier cohorts and have fun recalling the good old days.

The Eddlemans are reminded of their life on Lillie Street when they decorate their Christmas tree. Each holiday, Teddy carefully unpacks special ornaments dated December 1950-1955. They are keepsakes from the annual trim-the-tree parties they used to have when each friend was asked to bring an ornament.

Walt Kirk, one of Eddleman's friends in high school from Mount Vernon, Illinois, who later played basketball with him at Illinois and then in the pros, recalled those Zollner Pistons days. "In the early 1950s, the total outlay for salaries for the Pistons was about $100,000. That was for the entire team—not just one player! In those days, we felt we were being paid well. We were also given meal money, about $6-$8 per day. Our transportation costs were paid, and we usually traveled by train."

Dike and Kirk competed against each other since grade school, and they share many memories. "I recall the time we played in the Illinois vs. Indiana All-Star Basketball game. For many years, there had been a terrific rivalry between Illinois and Indiana over who had the better high school basketball teams. In 1942, the All-Star game was played in my hometown, Mount Vernon. Dike and I roomed together during the week, and I'll never forget that game. During the first half, Illinois was down by at least 10 or 12 points. During a second-half timeout, we all met under our basket. It was illegal to talk to your coach during timeouts at that point in basketball history. Dike convinced us to go to a full-court press for the final two quarters because that was the style of basketball he had played under Coach Trout. Thanks to Dike, Illinois came from behind to beat the Indiana All-Stars. Dike was a great competitor and a super guy! They may have been able to take the boy out of Southern Illinois, but they have never been able to take Southern Illinois out of the boy. His 'run and gun' style of play was exciting! He should serve as a role model for today's young players because he never let his fame go to his head."

Throughout his career, Dike tried to heed Coach Trout's advice to remain humble. It was flattering, though, when he was told about people who named their pets and their children after him. "I even had a colt (a trotter) as a namesake," Dike said. "His name was Dike Direct. He was the son of Billy Direct and Au Revoir. He was owned by K. R. and Dave Ward, great people in the insurance business from Bloomington, Illinois."

Two years after moving to Fort Wayne, Teddy was expecting. Dike was playing in Philadelphia on the night his second daughter, Nancy, was born. When Teddy called to say the baby was on its way, Dike was just leaving the hotel for the arena. He told Teddy to call their good friend, Barbara Schaus, wife of Pistons teammate Fred Schaus. Barb rushed Teddy to the hospital. Barb did a great job filling in for Dike. When the team returned, however, Barb told Dike, "Don't ever do that to me again!" December 18, 1952, was a special night for the Eddlemans. While

Dike labored on the hardwood, Teddy did the same in a hospital delivery room. Because Dike was on the road, heading for other Eastern destinations, an enlarged photograph was sent to him so he could get the first glimpse of his baby girl, Nancy Dru.

While playing for the Pistons, Dike cultivated an enduring friendship with Fred Schaus, who later became head coach for the Los Angeles Lakers. After leaving professional basketball, Schaus became head coach at Purdue. Schaus said Dike was a "natural" during their professional basketball days. "There was never a more fun-loving and sincere guy. We shared some great memories together. The thing I remember most about the 'Diker' is that he was the 'greatest all-around everything.' Whether it was punting a football a mile high or just hitting the hell out of a golf ball, he was a superb athlete and a great competitor. He was everybody's friend, and his charismatic personality drew others to him."

Life in Fort Wayne was fabulous for Teddy and Dike. They had healthy children, fantastic friends, a new car and a lovely home. Everything had been paid for with cash. Having lived through the Depression, Teddy and Dike shared the same philosophy on finances. If they couldn't pay cash, they couldn't afford to buy it. Even at the pinnacle of Dike's career, money never became his idol.

There was, however, the temptation to party. After games, it was dinner and drinks. Charged up from a night of physical contact, the players, along with their wives, went out for late dinners and tried to unwind.

During those later pro basketball years, keeping the home fires burning was tedious. Taking care of the children wasn't easy for Teddy. Sometimes the team was on the road for more than a week. Teddy recalled bundling up the children, even on stormy nights, for a trip to the airport to meet the Pistons' plane. The Pistons were the first pro basketball team to buy their own airplane. It sure beat riding the rails!

During his off-seasons in Indiana, Eddleman worked as recreational director for Central Soya Inc., a division of McMillen Feed Mills. While working in the Decatur office, Dike became friends with one of the tenured Soya secretaries, Amy Woodward. Amy owned a summer cottage on Indiana's Pretty Lake. During the warmer months, Amy invited the Eddleman family to the lake for weekends and holidays. While vacationing at Pretty Lake, Teddy and Dike met Buleah and Al Gratz. The Gratz lake house was next to Amy's. There always was plenty of action at the Gratz place. They had five boys: Tim, Tom, Terry and twins, Denny and Danny, who were Diana's age.

Dike loved to sit at the end of Amy's boat dock with his fishing pole. Teddy had her hands full chasing Nancy, who had developed some tomboy traits. If Nancy wasn't climbing a tree, she would be diving into the lake headfirst off Amy's pier.

An avid golfer, Dike usually packed his clubs for these excursions. He and Al Gratz hit golf balls off the shore's edge just for fun. Many a beer was bet on who could hit the longest drive into the lake.

Those summer and fall days at Pretty Lake were spent forming close bonds between family members and friends. Dike and his family returned to Fort Wayne from those lazy days at the lake looking tanned and well-rested.

Late in 1954, after learning he would be traded to the Baltimore Bullets, Dike retired from professional basketball at 32. "By this time, I had three young children and a wife to think about. My son, Tom, had been born on November 4, 1954, and all my traveling was putting a strain on my marriage. I felt I had to make a choice, and I chose to be with my family," Dike said.

Dike and Dr. Alan Chambers, the Pistons' team physician, developed a friendship that continued even after Dike retired from pro ball. "We went out to dinner with our wives one night," Dike said. "Doc started to kid me about picking up a few pounds. I suppose I had gained a little weight after I quit basketball. 'I bet you can't high jump 6 feet anymore,' he said to me. Well, you know how you always feel like you still have what it takes? I said I bet I *could*. Doc bet me a steak dinner that I couldn't."

The next day, they both went out to North Side, where the Pistons played, to use their high jump pit. "On the first try, I cleared 6 feet. I kept going until I hit 6 feet, 4 inches," Dike said. Ever the competitor, Dike still was meeting the challenge.

After accepting a full-time position with Central Soya, Dike lived in Fort Wayne, Indiana, until 1956, when he transferred to Gibson City, Illinois. There, he became the personnel director for one of the company's soybean processing plants, Soya's second largest. Little did this former Fighting Illini realize that this transfer would be the first step toward his journey back home.

CHAPTER 10

A MOVE TO GIBSON CITY, ILLINOIS

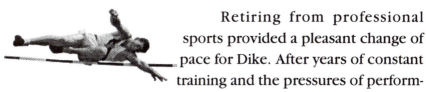 Retiring from professional sports provided a pleasant change of pace for Dike. After years of constant training and the pressures of performing, Dike sought security, peace of mind and some well-deserved rest and relaxation. He found all of these in the small town where he transferred.

In summer 1956, the Eddlemans moved to Gibson City, a small rural community in Central Illinois with a population of about 3,600. Located 30 miles north of his college alma mater, Gibson City was a wonderful place to rear a young family. Moving back to their home state appealed to Teddy and Dike because they would be closer to their relatives in Centralia.

Comfortable in any social setting, the Eddlemans established friendships and found small-town life enjoyable. They purchased a home at the northern edge of town. Their neighbors to the east were Dr. and Mrs. Earl Bucher. Neighbors to the west included Dr. and Mrs. Ed Etherton and Dick Moody.

Dick and Geri Walter became their closest friends. Dick Walter was the manager of the Central Soya plant in Gibson City. The Walters also had three children, Patty, Mike and Andy. In Dick and Geri, Dike and Teddy met their social match. There were cookouts, potlucks, picnics—you name it! These two families never missed an opportunity to get together.

True to their congenial nature, the Eddlemans and the Walters became infamous for throwing outstanding parties for their friends. These affairs usually were planned around a unique theme requiring costumes. With Teddy's knack for clever ideas and detail, these galas were raving successes. The family photo albums are filled with pictures of guests dressed like little "kids", cowboys, Indians and hula dancers.

Dike and Dick were like brothers. Both of them shared a wonderful sense of humor, and they spent lots of time together. Dick had a company car. He would bring Dike home for lunch every day and pick him up like clockwork an hour later. After drinking a can of chocolate Metracal (the diet drink of the day) for lunch, Dike usually would lie on the living room sofa until he heard Dick honk for their return trip to the office. This thoughtful act of kindness freed the use of the family car for Teddy during the days of single-car families.

Public relations was definitely Dike's strong suit. Whether he was talking to the gals in the coffee shop or the CEO of the parent company, Dike made people smile. He often gave his close friends nicknames that made them feel unique and at ease.

As personnel manager, Dike oversaw the plant's 600 employees. He liked the individuals with whom he worked. He never complained about his job. Every night, he shared some story at the dinner table about the day's events. It was at those evening meals that it became apparent to his family that he was a good listener, too.

Central Soya treated its employees well. One of Dike's responsibilities was to plan the annual company Christmas party at the local high school gym. There always would be some sort of entertainment. After the show, each family would bring home a burlap sack full of toys and candy. These parties were on Saturday evenings. The Eddlemans and the Walters spent that day stuffing each bag with the appropriate toys according to the tags that listed the names and ages of the recipient family members. Dike sometimes put extra items into some of the bags. "This may be all the Christmas presents this family gets," Dike said.

Teddy and Dike always have been an affectionate couple. Teddy used to kiss Dike before work each morning and greeted him the same way every night. Watching their 6-3 father sweep their 5-1 mother off her feet for a warm embrace is an image that fondly is remembered by the Eddleman children.

Although Dike and Teddy had their share of marital woes, they always worked through them. They discovered the essential ingredient necessary for a successful marriage: commitment. Communication also was a key element in keeping their relationship stable and happy. Through trust and respect, Dike and Teddy developed a profoundly loving experience that has endured the test of time. Several common bonds have helped solidify their marriage. Besides a passion for sports, they share a belief in God, a love of children, a zest for living and a sense of humor.

Teddy and Dike said their faith in God has provided them with a source of strength and comfort throughout their lives. Having been reared in Christian homes, Teddy and Dike's religion has served as a paradigm. Sports editor Fred Young published a full-page ad with a letter written by a much younger Eddleman in *The Bloomington Pantagraph* on July 11, 1948. In it, Dike wrote,

> Sunday school and church play an important part in the life of any man—particularly in an athlete, because he is thus directed in the right channels.
>
> The older I get and the farther I go in life, the more I realize that I owe much to my early training in Sunday school and church. I was thrown into the right environment — and my associates were men of ideals.

I learned in Sunday school that jealousies only tend to break up teams and destroy teamwork. There is no factor so important to a team's success as the willingness to work together.

I learned to love my fellow men, work with them, rather than against them. I learned what humility, tolerance, and faith mean. I was fortunate to work under a great Christian gentleman, Arthur L. Trout, throughout my high school days. He has made a record in his years at Centralia that will be felt through another generation!

You have to have a clean mind and body to succeed in athletics. You'll make no mistake, boys, in attending Sunday school and church. Both have contributed largely to my own success in athletics.

                                     Signed,
                                     Dwight "Dike" Eddleman

No endorsements were offered for writing the letter. Dike wrote it because he felt in his heart it was the right thing to do. He feels the same way today. "My faith in God and a good sense of humor have helped me through many of life's crises."

An episode that illustrates the Eddlemans' sense of humor and their love for their children occurred one Sunday morning at the First Christian Church in Gibson City where Dike was serving as a deacon. Teddy and the children were seated among the congregation as communion was passed. As is the tradition of that denomination, the deacons pass symbols of the body and blood of Christ for members to partake as they are seated in the pews. As the organist played a communion hymn, heads were bowed in silence. Just as the deacons and elders came forward to distribute the communion trays, the silence was broken by the young, but very distinct, voice of four-year-old Tom Eddleman, who exclaimed, "Look, Mom! Here comes Dad with the drinks!" Needless to say, the pews shook as the congregation tried to contain its laughter. Even Reverend McDormand was smiling! Young Tommy never figured out what was so funny.

The Eddlemans' love for children has been apparent throughout their lives. Besides spending time with their children, they also have volunteered endless hours to youth activities. Chuck Flynn, former sports information director at the University of Illinois and sports editor of the Champaign-Urbana *News-Gazette,* recalled Dike's willingness to give demonstrations around Illinois. "I traveled a lot with Dike about the state. Wherever we went, he always found time to go to the high school athletic department, gather a few track men and stage a demonstration in high-jumping. Even years after Dike had finished competition, he could clear 6 feet or better. While youngsters stood bug-eyed, he'd show them how it was done. What a fine influence he was to young athletes for many years. Dike always had words of encouragement and coaching tips for aspiring athletes or 'the champions of the future' as he called them."

Backed by the support and sponsorship of Central Soya Inc., Eddleman organized and promoted the Wildcat Little League baseball program for Gibson City youths. Dike also officiated football and basketball games throughout the state. He often paired up with his friend, Bob Royal, who traveled extensively with him in the 1960s. Certainly no one doubted Dike's qualifications as an official, but several of his officiating buddies noted that Dike often directed more attention to the audience than to the players. Many fans seated in the bleachers waved and spoke to Dike while he worked a game. He always acknowledged them.

Bill Vangel, football coach and basketball official, said, "During one of Dike's last years of 'ref-ing', we did a basketball game together in Tuscola. We put the ball in play, and I ran up the sideline. I looked across the gym to find Dike, and there he was, shaking hands with some of the guys in the stands. I jokingly asked him after the game if he was running for public office!"

Eddleman claimed he officiated games to stay in shape. The extra money he made also was an incentive. Although Dike never complained about the driving or the late nights, Teddy stayed awake until Dike arrived home. On nights when the weather was bad, Teddy stood at the living room windows awaiting Dike's safe return.

Besides being a full-time housewife and mother, Teddy donated her time as a Girl Scout and a Cub Scout leader. She served as president of the PTA, president of the Woman's Club, president of the Women's Hospital Auxiliary and president of the Christian Women's Fellowship. She was the first woman to serve on the Gibson City Community Hospital Board. For her efforts, she was honored as the 1979 Gibson City Citizen of the Year.

After moving from Gibson City, Teddy continued her volunteer work as president of the Champaign-Urbana Women's Club. She also served as an officer on the state board of the General Federation of Women's Clubs.

Teddy and Dike always made time for their four children. Teddy provided Dike with three daughters, Diana, Nancy and Kristy, and one son, Tom. Their youngest child, Kristy Ann, was born on October 16, 1964.

Since there is a 10-year difference between Tom and Kristy, Teddy was concerned when her last pregnancy was confirmed. She was 39 years old in 1964. Dr. Earl Bucher, the Eddlemans' neighbor, was Teddy's physician, and Dr. Paul Sunderland delivered the baby. Doc Bucher eased Teddy's anxiety by telling her this was God's way of showing her what a wonderful mother she was. He told Teddy that she was being given a special gift. These comforting words, however, provided little consolation to Dike and Teddy.

The Eddlemans lived only three blocks from the hospital. Late one evening, Teddy went into labor with Kristy. The next morning, Teddy and Dike had a daughter. Kristy and Teddy were hospitalized for more than a week because the baby was delivered by Cesarean section. Tom, Nancy and Diana were eager to see their new sibling. One evening after dinner, they walked to the hospital. Tom and Nancy stood beneath Teddy's hospital room window and yelled for her. Meantime, Diana ran to Jim and Marti Hager's house to borrow a ladder. The children took turns climbing to the second-floor window and sneaking a peek at the baby. They also blew kisses to Teddy, who started crying when they left. Doc Bucher was right. Kristy was healthy, and she was precious!

There was never a dull moment for the Eddlemans. Teddy and Dike encouraged their children to excel as individuals. They didn't pressure the children to conform to their interests. This especially was true for Tom. The only son of an outstanding athlete, Tom undoubtedly felt a great deal of pressure to perform athletically. Luckily, Tom was a good athlete in his own right. With little coaching or encouragement from Dike, Tom excelled as a punter, kicker, wide receiver and linebacker for the Gibson City Greyhounds. Tom's high school coach, Ron Metz, said, "Tom's sport was football. I remember he had a great kick during a game against Clifton Central. We 'lost' the ball up in the lights that night because he kicked it so high. I believe it was a 79-yarder. Dike was at that game. I'll never forget it. It was a great night for Tom."

Tom also participated in track and basketball. He played football at the University of Illinois until he was sidelined with a knee injury. Following in his father's footsteps, Tom married his high school sweetheart, Lynn Tyler.

Nancy was a fun-loving and energetic child. Homecoming attendant, cheerleader and everybody's friend, that was Nancy. After college, she became a flight attendant for Continental Airlines until her daughters were born. The little tomboy with the auburn ringlets grew up to be a tireless volunteer and a devoted mother.

Kristy, the youngest daughter, was everyone's darling. After Tom graduated from high school, Kristy was like an only child. When the Eddlemans' oldest children were growing up, the family took trips to Daytona Beach, Florida in a Chevy Impala with no air conditioning. When Kristy was growing up, her family vacations were flights to Acapulco and Hawaii. She loved flying! Maybe that's why she became a flight attendant. That cute little bundle of joy grew up to become a real beauty. The most distinguishing characteristic about Kristy is that she is not only beautiful on the outside, but she has a lovely personality, too.

Appreciated for their differences in temperament and disposition, all four of the Eddleman children grew up feeling safe and secure in Gibson City. There were great times spent together as a family. There always was the sound of laughter around the house. With the help of their parents, the Eddleman offspring learned how to fish with a bamboo pole, swim in a lake, walk down a beach, read a good book and plant a seed. Such invaluable lessons have helped them understand what truly is significant. Their parents taught them to enjoy life's simple pleasures. All four agree they wouldn't trade their childhood days for anything. These memories become more special as time passes.

The Eddlemans have seven grandchildren. Many have asked, "Will there ever be another Dike Eddleman?" Perhaps not, for he appears to be one in a million. However, among his grandchildren, Dike has two namesakes. They are Dwight Edward Eddleman and Thomas Wayne Eddleman, who reside in Champaign, Illinois, the sons of Thomas Dwight Eddleman Jr. and his wife, Lynn. Nancy Dru Hambright, and her husband, Randy, live in San Antonio, Texas, with their two daughters, Georgie Dru and Anna Elizabeth. Diana Eddleman Lenzi, and her husband, Gene, live in Tuscola, Illinois, with her three children, Brittany Crawford, John Crawford (Beau) and Blair Eddleman Wilson. The youngest Eddleman daughter, Kristy Ann, resides in Orlando, Florida, where she is based as a flight attendant for Delta Airlines. Although sports appeared to be an all-consuming factor in Dike's life, his family always came first.

Teddy said Dike always has been a keen judge of character. It has been like a sixth sense to Dike and has helped him immensely in public relations. He also possesses a special gift for remembering names and faces. An example comes from Chuck Holt, attorney and former member of the Centralia High School track squad, who recalled meeting Eddleman in Centralia in the late 1960s when Holt was in high school. "When I was introduced to Dike for the first time, I felt honored, having lived next to Coach Jimmie Evers and having heard so many stories of the legendary Dwight Eddleman. After our introduction, I was shocked when the first thing Dike did was congratulate *me* on my track times which he had read about in the *Centralia Sentinel* that morning. I felt about 10 feet tall receiving a compliment from someone of his caliber who remembered my name and my accomplishment! What a guy!" Making others feel special has been a gift that has enhanced Dike's personal and professional life.

While living in Gibson City, Dike continued to schedule speaking engagements. He passed out cards printed by Central Soya to his audiences. They were titled "Food For Thought" and read as follows:

The Great Sin	FEAR
The Best Day	TODAY
The Best Town	WHERE YOU SUCCEED
The Best Work	WHAT YOU LIKE
The Best Play	WORK
The Greatest Stumbling Block	EGOTISM
The Greatest Mistake	GIVING UP
The Most Expensive Indulgence	HATE
The Greatest Troublemaker	ONE WHO TALKS TOO MUCH
The Most Ridiculous Trait	FALSE PRIDE
The Most Dangerous Man	THE LIAR
The Greatest Need	COMMON SENSE
The Greatest Thought	GOD
The Cleverest Man	ONE WHO ALWAYS DOES WHAT HE THINKS IS RIGHT

BE A CLEVER MAN

On the front of each card it said: "This day I will beat my own record." These words encompass Dike's philosophy.

Working side by side in management during their tenure with Central Soya, Walter and Eddleman kept the soybean processing plant free from union affiliation for 13 years. The 14th year would not prove as successful. After a bitter campaign that included threatening telephone calls, the words "vote union" painted on Eddleman's house and Pinkerton guards posted outside the Eddleman home, the union won in a close election. This defeat was an emotional blow to Dike. Later that year, Dike was offered and accepted a job with the University of Illinois Foundation, its fund-raising entity. Although Dike found his work with Central Soya gratifying and his lifestyle in Gibson City comfortable, when opportunity knocked in 1969, Dike enthusiastically opened the door.

CHAPTER 11

RETURNING HOME TO HIS ALMA MATER

With encouragement from fellow Illini Gene Lamb and Red Pace, Dike accepted the job as associate director of the University of Illinois Grants-in-Aid program in the summer of 1969. His work developed into a labor of love as he encountered Illini alumni and friends nationwide. Eddleman eagerly returned to his alma mater, which provided him with numerous athletic and academic opportunities. He came home to serve a program that provides financial aid for student-athletes. His motivation: to help others have the same opportunity that he had.

The University of Illinois created a fund-raising organization to provide scholarships for its student-athletes because of the ever-increasing tuition costs and expanding athletic budgets. In 1970, Dike spearheaded these fund-raising efforts that began in the late 1950s.

At the 1952 National Collegiate Athletic Association Convention, a 12-Point Code was adopted for intercollegiate athletics. The purpose was to regulate the number and amount of financial grants given to athletes by an institution. Before, there were great inequities in the amount of aid given to college athletes. Through the 12-Point Code, the NCAA imposed limits on scholarships. Colleges and universities developed their own programs for raising and allocating funds in accordance with the NCAA's rules and regulations.

The University of Illinois did not initiate its Grants-In-Aid program until 1958. Before, money contributed to the university for athletic financial aid was managed subjectively. Records rarely were kept because there was no designated department to oversee these funds.

The Grants-In-Aid program originated at the Champaign-Urbana campus when administrators saw the need to establish a fund to aid various extracurricular programs. During the early 1960s, financial support for non-athletic programs was dropped. The Grants-In-Aid program began concentrating solely on raising funds for athletics. Records were kept for the first time in 1967 when $119,500 was contributed.

John "Red" Pace was the executive director for the Grants-In-Aid program from 1958 until 1970. When Pace retired, Eddleman was appointed his successor. Dike thoroughly enjoyed his work for the university, which entailed a lot of traveling. Dike's game plan consisted of flying with the football team to away games, attending alumni brunches, luncheons, dinners and cocktail parties. He also appointed 10 statewide district chairmen, made presentations, solicited funds through the mail and hosted tailgates at football games. He held about 30 golf outings a year for Grants-In-Aid and Varsity I members, the organization comprised of former Illinois varsity lettermen. In the late 1970s, Eddleman was driving 60,000 to 70,000 miles a year asking people to contribute to Illinois' largest educational institution.

Lou Henson, former head basketball coach at the University of Illinois, traveled with Dike to many Grants-In-Aid functions. "In the spring of 1975 when I joined the U. of I. Athletic Association as head basketball coach, Dike was considered, and remains so in the minds of many, to be the best all-around performer in the history of Illinois sports," Henson said. "I soon discovered that I would be traveling with Dike around the state to participate in numerous Grants-In-Aid fund-raisers. My first thought was that such an accomplished athlete may be a little on the arrogant side. It was quite to the contrary as I learned upon our initial introduction. I was delighted that my Oklahoma heritage served me well by providing me with the apt description of this Illinois sports hero as a 'good ole' boy. The phrase still fits. I'll let others more knowledgeable describe Dike's remarkable past athletic feats. I'll just tell it as I now see it — that throughout this great state of Illinois, Dike Eddleman remains the best beloved Illini athlete to don the Orange and Blue."

When Eddleman joined the university, he was placed with the University of Illinois Foundation and given an office on the third floor of the Illini Union. Dike and his secretary, Janell Hartley, handled all the Grants-In-Aid business. George Legg was in charge of the Varsity I Men's Association. A unique component of the Illinois scholarship program, the Fighting Illini Pork Club, was developed. The Illinois Pork Producers' Association teams with the Grants-In-Aid to raise funds by sponsoring a Pork Day during one football Saturday each season. Much of the organization's groundwork was laid by Fran and Elaine Callahan. Jimmy Dean even visited the U. of I. campus with his sausage and pigskin jackets!

Dike said the Illini traditions are family traditions. He promoted that concept during his fund-raising efforts. Perhaps nowhere is the family spirit more evident than at the football tailgates hosted by the Eddlemans. The Eddleman children and grandchildren all have scrapbooks with their first Illini tailgate pictures pasted in them for posterity.

Teddy is probably *the* authority on tailgate parties. Teddy said, "There is a very good reason why they rope off Dike's parking space on the west side of the stadium by Gate 22 on game day. For years, Dike and I have been greeting, feeding and collecting checks from Grant-In-Aiders at the trunk of our car. People often wondered why Dike always wore a shirt and sports jacket to the football games instead of sweat shirts or more casual attire. The truth is that Dike was really working at those games. He would come home with all kinds of checks in his pockets. I always had to be careful to look in his pockets so that none of the Grants-In-Aid checks would go through the washer!"

The Eddlemans started their tailgate parties by inviting 10 or 12 people. "As the years passed, more and more people showed up. Some were already contributing and just wanted to visit with Dike; some weren't contributing to the program but wanted to know more about it. It was typical for Dike to come home from a football game with thousands of dollars worth of Grants-In-Aid checks in his pockets. Over the years, many interesting people have ventured by our parking spot. There was Artie Johnson, an Illini alum, famous for the television show 'Laugh In' and his lovely wife, Giesela. Bob Hope, Dick Butkus, McLean Stevenson, Brent Musburger, Jimmy Dean, Governor Jim Thompson and Governor Jim Edgar were just a few of the celebrities who stopped by." Although such guests added excitement to football Saturdays, Teddy and Dike enjoyed their "true blue" Illini friends most.

Teddy said she has hosted more than 200 tailgate parties the past 27 years, including some at out-of-town games. Thanks to her dear friends, who often attended the away games with her, she didn't have to do all the work. She loved planning them!

Although Illini fans come in all shapes and sizes, they all have one obsession, their game-day apparel. No true-blue Illini fan would be caught dead at a football tailgate party without his or her orange-and-blue attire. Teddy always hated for cold weather to arrive because those clever creations would be covered with coats.

After decades of choosing orange-and-blue outfits, some days it was difficult for Teddy to come up with something different. She got tired of dressing in those same colors. Teddy recalled a game at Wisconsin when she, Marty Thomson and Charlene Cain were walking to the car after an Illini victory. A Wisconsin fan looked at them and said, "They look like pumpkins." Another Badger fan piped up, "They're shaped like pumpkins, too!" After that incident, Teddy tried to wear navy blue whenever possible.

Planning the tailgate menus provided a challenge. Teddy searched through cookbooks for days trying to come up with something different. Sometimes, it got pretty bizarre. One season, she made orange-and-blue deviled eggs. They were simple to make, and they caught everyone's attention.

One thing that amazed Teddy was how people liked to drink alcohol and eat cookies and brownies. One funny tailgating incident involved Alexander "Stringer" Bush of Manhattan, Illinois. He always came to Teddy and Dike's tailgate. Being a good contributor to the university, he always was welcome. One Saturday, he was especially hungry. After the game "Stringer" came back to Dike's car and said, "Teddy, may I have some more of your delicious brownies?" She said, "Here!" "Stringer" proceeded to pick up the pan of brownies and began walking to his car. Teddy turned to Dike and said, "There goes 'Stringer' with my brownies and my favorite baking pan!" Dike just smiled and said, "He must have liked them, honey."

Tailgating had become a way of life each fall. As the number of guests grew, Teddy tried to serve something different. She went from ham sandwiches to chili dogs to bratwurst to chicken. Kentucky Fried Chicken must have loved her when she finally decided to place a standing order with it. This made life on Saturday game days much easier. Never knowing how many Illini would stop by for food and drinks was a problem. Bless Carlene Wilkens' heart! She was in charge of feeding the press box personnel on game days. She must have looked down on the parking lot and saw Teddy struggling to feed 40 people with three buckets of chicken. Carlene never failed to send down some of those delicious pork sandwiches provided by the Fighting Illini Pork Club.

One nice thing that happened because of Dike and Teddy's many years of tailgating was having that parking spot roped off. It was much easier to tell people to come down in front of Gate 22 on the west side of Memorial Stadium than to search for them in the sea of orange and blue on football Saturdays. The Eddlemans tried to arrive at the lot at least four hours (sometimes more) before game time. Bob Minsker almost always beat them there. Teddy always laughed when she and Dike drove up. Bob would have his piece of indoor-outdoor carpeting in place, his table already set and his grill fired up!

Teddy said she and Dike made many friends through tailgating. These friendships have grown through the years. She always had plenty of help from Marty and Will Thomson (from Galva, Illinois) or Charlene Cain (from Highland, Illinois), or Sharon Wade (from Carlyle, Illinois). Teddy often traveled with these friends to away games when Dike traveled with the team. The trips to away games always were winners whether the Illini won or lost.

Traveling to Wisconsin was a favorite trip for Teddy because she and her Illini tailgaters stopped in New Glaris, Wisconsin. There, they met a fine gentleman, Otto Puempel. He owned Puempel's Tavern, which had been operated by his family since the 1800s. Beautiful handpainted murals decorated the walls, and the tavern's focal point was a highly polished mahogany bar. Otto always seemed happy that the Illini fans returned biennially. He greeted them with German beer, cheeses, Braunschweiger and German mustard. On one trip, some of the women were so impressed with the mustard that they decided to buy some as they left New Glaris. Stopping at a local grocery store, four of them picked up an armload of jars each and stood in line to check out. As they stood there in their orange-and-blue garb, a man standing behind them in the checkout line said, "Ladies, don't they sell mustard in Illinois?"

Perhaps the greatest thing about the tailgating experience was Teddy's contribution to Dike's job. A loyal wife, Teddy always has been there to support Dike's efforts. Although her decisions on what kind and how much food to serve may not appear monumental, the important thing was Dike and Teddy always worked together as a team. Rain or shine, he could count on her. Their relationship was strengthened working side by side.

The monumental task of covering the state in search of contributors took more than tailgate parties. A Chicago office was opened in 1979 under the direction of current Athletic Director Ron Guenther. A year later, Wayne Williams was named to head an office in St. Louis. Maintaining an office on campus, Dike coordinated all Illinois Grants-In-Aid activities. Eddleman said his first team of district chairmen included: I. Robert Rylowicz, Chicago; II. Robert Thornton, Joliet; III. Wayne Baird, Broadview; IV. Will Thomson, Galva; V. Richard Ware, Jacksonville; VI. Robert "Bo" Batchelder, Peoria; VII. Gene Lamb, Champaign; VIII. Stanley Funk, Springfield; IX. David Lembke, Mascoutah; and X. Willard (Bill) Franks, Harrisburg.

In 1978, Eddleman moved to a trailer next to the Assembly Hall. Dike affectionately called the trailer the "Little House on the Prairie", an appropriate name because there was no indoor plumbing! Dike received excellent secretarial assistance from Rene Nelson and Jayne Valek. Jayne is the daughter of Jim Valek, former U. of I. football player and coach. During the "trailer days", Bill Butkovich, a former Fighting Illini athlete, took over the Varsity I Men's position.

Under Eddleman's guidance, the G-I-A pursued two short-term and two long-term goals. The short-term goals were: 1) To continue to build the base of support for the G-I-A program through annual contributions and 2) To increase the benefits that G-I-A contributors received. Throughout his years as a fundraiser, Eddleman was dedicated to bringing more people into the program and encouraging present contributors to increase their support. Eddleman said G-I-A contributors deserved special benefits such as invitations to golf outings, luncheons, dinners and cocktail parties where key personalities in the athletic department would make appearances to promote communication between the university and its supporters.

In 1983, various clubs were formed that allowed large contributors an opportunity to receive preferred seating at basketball and football games (plus special parking privileges for those events) when they purchased season tickets. This system listed six clubs a supporter could join, depending on the amount he contributed. The contributions ranged from $100 for the Tomahawk Club to $3,000 for the Tribal Council. The Chief Club and the Tribal Council contributors received the most benefits for gifts of $1,000 and $3,000, respectively.

The two long-term goals of the G-I-A program were: 1) To establish an endowment program that would raise enough capital to provide funding for new facilities and take some of the pressure off the G-I-A program and 2) To identify the major gift contributors and bring these individuals closer to the program.

Through G-I-A, Eddleman and the athletic department developed a system of giving that enabled supporters to contribute gifts in six ways: 1) cash gifts; 2) gifts-in-kind; 3) livestock or other food items; 4) endowment scholarships; 5) gifts of stock; and 6) matching gifts. Cash gifts were the most popular, and the money went directly to the athletic programs. The second method, the gift-in-kind, helped defray athletic department expenditures by providing goods and services in lieu of cash. Such gifts included building materials, services, carpeting, hotel rooms and other commodities. The third method, livestock and food items, was used to feed the athletes. A fourth method, the endowment scholarship, was designed for large contributors who wanted a scholarship established in their name. The fifth category included gifts of stock, securities and/or real estate, which provided a more creative avenue to contribute. Matching gifts involved a program where businessmen matched their employees' contributions, usually on a 1:1 or 2:1 ratio.

Under Athletic Director John Mackovic, the G-I-A program was renamed the Fighting Illini Scholarship Fund (F-I-S-F) in 1990 and placed under the auspices of the Division of Intercollegiate Athletics. This resulted from the reorganization of the Athletic Association. Eddleman's office again changed locations. He moved to a suite on the 17th floor of the University Inn. With this move came a new challenge for Dike and his secretary, Louita Hartwell. Louita has shown an initiative and a finesse that has eased Dike's workload.

There is a mutual admiration between Dike and his secretary. "I must admit that when my friend, Jayne Valek, became Dike's secretary, I didn't know who he was. She just couldn't believe that! In 1983 when Jayne decided to move to South Carolina, Dike asked me to be his secretary," Louita said. "It was the easiest and best decision I ever made. During the many years I've worked for Dike, we've seen many changes in the athletic department—from administration changes to coaching staff changes to becoming a part of the university. Dike never changes. He is every secretary's dream. He is so easy to work for and always appreciates everything you do for him, including the little things. He has always made the work environment fun for his entire staff. We always work hard for him. It has been an honor and a pleasure to be part of his team. If there were more men like Dike in the world—the world would be a much better place to live. Now I'm surprised when I find someone from the state of Illinois who doesn't know Dike!"

Most contributors think the Fighting Illini Scholarship Fund's success can be attributed to Dike's efforts. According to Seely Johnston, Dike's success can be attributed to one word: "Trust. People trust Dike because of his professional integrity."

Perhaps the most important aspect of Eddleman's affiliation with the University of Illinois is that he has not selfishly taken without giving in return. The late Bill Butler, Dike's longtime friend and a Fighting Illini Scholarship Fund supporter, summed up Eddleman's career when he said: "His athletic heroics and name recognition may open many doors, but Dike has many donors giving to Illinois just because of him. People want to do something for the 'Diker'. Because of his enthusiasm and energy, they want to help him. There will never be another representative as loyal and dedicated to the University of Illinois as Dike Eddleman. Hail to the 'Chief'."

Ben Crackel, Dike's close friend since college, bears witness to Dike's drive toward excellence. "His dedication in sports showed in so many ways. I remember at day's end after working for eight hours, he would head for the high jump pits to practice, usually until dark. Many times I stayed to help put up the bar after each jump. I remember how he used to practice kicking the football by himself well into dark or when the weather forced him inside, heading to Huff Gym to shoot baskets. People all over the state and throughout the nation support the F-I-S-F, not only because they support Illinois—but because they are showing faith in a program headed by Illinois' greatest athlete and friend!"

According to Eddleman, no gift was too small. He treated all contributions equally. Whether he was having tea with a widow in Indiana, a woman who called him annually to give a generous check, or whether he was visiting a retired gentleman whose small contribution, in proportion to his worth, was like a gift of thousands, Dike was equally appreciative.

Will Thomson, a University of Illinois graduate and a former Illini track standout, described Eddleman's enthusiasm. "I have seen him make phone call after phone call just to locate two tickets for someone who had just joined this program. Dike would say to me, 'Will, you never know. Some day this guy may have the means to be a larger part of our program and, quite possibly, our largest contributor.' Dike is an excellent judge of character and an eternal optimist! I've seen him drive 400 miles after work to make a speech, for no money of course, just to promote the university and its athletic program. He invariably would be back home that night to be with Teddy and the family. It's not always easy to go to a restaurant, a banquet or an athletic event with Dike. You just never know how long it's going to take you to get from the door to your seat. He knows everybody. Everybody knows him. And he speaks to them all."

Eddleman has worked with many outstanding personalities including Ray Eliot, John "Red" Pace, Gene Vance, George Legg, John Corbally, Stan Ikenberry and Morton Weir. It seems only fitting that his life has come full circle. The late John Watkins, manager of the 1947 University of Illinois basketball team and former owner of Delbert's Clothing Store in Arthur, Illinois, said, "He came to Champaign a country boy wearing rolled-up blue jeans and flannel shirts, and he left a 'Dapper Dan'."

Lou Tepper, former head football coach for the University of Illinois, said Dike's competitive spirit gave him an edge. "I first came to the University of Illinois in 1988. One of my first recollections of Dike was what I had read in some of our record books. Dike Eddleman still had the record for the longest punt at Illinois. He also had the longest punt return in Illinois' storied history. That really struck me. 'Wow! What an athlete this guy must be!' I didn't yet know of Dike's illustrious career. Those two things really struck me as to the kind of athletic ability we were talking about. I can tell you that after getting to know Dike, the quality that impresses all of us is the great humility that he possesses. At every stop on our F-I-S-F caravan, the people stand and applaud the greatness of Dike Eddleman. Part of that is due to what they have witnessed and read about his athletic exploits. But more important to them is the way in which he carries himself as such a gentleman with such great humility. In his mid-70s, he's still a great competitor. I'm just a 'hacker' at golf, but we played nine holes together on a very challenging course in 1992. He was nothing but encouraging to me. We finally got to this long par 5. I was sitting on the green in four and Dike was sitting within chipping distance in two. He said, 'Go ahead, Lou, and putt for the par!' I made it, and you would have thought we had just won the Rose Bowl! He was so excited about seeing me get my first par. But the great part of this story is that on the next stroke, he chipped it in for an eagle! After my greatest golf game ever, with two par holes in a row, Dike still beat me by two strokes!"

Dike Eddleman is held in high esteem by many. A winning combination of charisma and talent has helped Eddleman accrue a long list of honors. He has been selected as a charter member of the Centralia Sports Hall of Fame and the Drake Relays Hall of Fame. He has been inducted into the Illinois Sports Hall of Fame, the Illinois Basketball Coaches' Hall of Fame, the Tri-State (Illinois, Indiana and Kentucky) Hall of Fame and the National High School Sports Hall of Fame. He was selected as a member of the University of Illinois All-Century Football Team, the *USA Today* All-Time Final Four Basketball Team and the *Chicago Tribune* All-Time All-Illinois Basketball Team. At the University of Illinois, he was a member of the Tribe of Illini, Ma-Wan-Da, Atius-Sachem and Chi Gamma lota (a veteran's honorary). In 1983, Eddleman was honored as the University of Illinois Varsity I Man of the Year. In 1993, Dike Eddleman was honored as the 59th Champaign-Urbana Exchange Club Golden Deed Award Recipient for his inspiration and service to others. Governor Jim Edgar has appointed him a member of the State Athletic Board.

Each selection has thrilled Dike. However, his induction into the Illinois Sports Hall of Fame in 1961 is perhaps his most prestigious honor because he joined an elite group of athletic greats including Amos Alonzo Stagg, Bob Zuppke, Red Grange, Walter Eckersall, George Halas, Bob Richards, Clark Griffith, Lou Boudreau, Al Spalding, Chick Evans, Charles Comiskey, George A. Huff, George Mikan and Otto Graham.

Lou Boudreau, former Fighting Illini great and baseball Hall of Famer, said, "I certainly hope that someday I can be as nice as Dike! He's tremendous—one of the finest loyal Illini that we have. I don't know of any other individual who could have done the job that Dike has done, and I hope he will continue to do, for the University of Illinois. Dike was a great athlete and the follow-

ing that he has—not only with Illini, but people all over the country—is incredible. No one is more personable than Dike. He has
a personality that everybody just grabs onto!"

Working for the U. of I. Foundation from 1969 to 1977,
Eddleman generated an increase in contributions from $145,000
to $500,000 annually. After moving Dike's office within the Ath-
letic Association in 1977, the scholarship program topped $1
million by 1980. When Dike retired on January 1, 1993, contributions surpassed $3 million annually.

If Eddleman had been born 20 years later, he might have
earned a million-dollar contract in the pros. Yet, Dike has no
regrets. Eddleman settled for the simple life. He fell in love with
his high school sweetheart, who has been cheering him on ever
since. He was content to extend his sports career for five seasons as an NBA player. He became a devoted father to his four
adoring children. He became an exemplary role model in his
professional life. Dike Eddleman is a million-dollar man. In his
tenure at the University of Illinois, Dike raised more than $45
million for his beloved university. Dike said his life has been
blessed, and there is no amount of money that could replace his
million memories, loving family and wonderful friends.

To honor his official retirement from the University of Illi-
nois, November 21, 1992, was proclaimed Dike Eddleman Day at
Memorial Stadium. At the Friday, November 13, 1992 Board of
Trustees' meeting, the board adopted a resolution commending
Dike's years of service. In part, the proclamation read:

> WHEREAS, Dwight "Dike" Eddleman earned 11 Fighting Illini
> varsity letters in three sports, football, basketball and track;
> AND WHEREAS, Dike Eddleman was possibly the greatest all-
> around athlete in the history of University of Illinois athletics;
> AND WHEREAS, Dike Eddleman, as executive director of the
> Fighting Illini Scholarship Fund since 1969, was instrumental
> in the increase of contributions for varsity athletic programs

during his tenure from $145,000 per year to nearly $3 million annually;

NOW, THEREFORE, the Board of Trustees of the University of Illinois hereby recognizes and commends the outstanding achievements of Dwight "Dike" Eddleman in representing the University both in athletics and in the administration of its athletic programs.

Signed,

Stanley O. Ikenberry

After the Illinois-Michigan State football game, 500 guests gathered at a banquet to pay tribute to Dike. Throughout the video replay of Dike's life, Teddy and Dike sat together on the stage, holding hands at times, reliving their exciting years together. Terry Fossum, Michigan State University's fund-raising representative, presented Dike with a set of Ping golf clubs from his fellow Big Ten colleagues. The tempo for the evening was set by former sportscaster Larry Stewart, the master of ceremonies. Morton Weir, University of Illinois chancellor, and Ken Boyle, University of Illinois trustee, presented plaques and proclamations. Athletic Director Ron Guenther referred to Dike as "Illinois' living legend" and praised Eddleman as his sports idol. He then announced the Athlete of the Year Award would be renamed the Dike Eddleman Athlete of the Year Award and presented him with a design of the new trophy to be awarded each spring in his honor. Bill Hopper, president of the F-I-S-F Advisory Board, made the surprise presentation of the evening when the Eddlemans were given the keys to a new navy blue Lumina. Bob Winchester, representing the Secretary of State's Office, unveiled the license plates for the new car that read "Chief 40." After a well-deserved vacation, Eddleman rejoined the Division of Intercollegiate Athletics as a consultant, continuing the job he has performed in the true Illini spirit. He moved his office again. It is now on the first floor of the Bielfeldt Athletic Administration Building.

It is reassuring to know that in a rapidly changing world, some traditions will be held forever dear. When the early French explorers paddled from Lake Michigan down nearby rivers, they found natives there who called themselves Illini or Illiniwek, which means "Superior Men." The Illiniwek were expert archers and swift runners. The French explorers subsequently called this area Illinois. From this heritage, the University of Illinois derives its name. Therefore, it is fitting that its students and alumni also are called Illini. It is in the spirit of Illini past and present that the accomplishments of Thomas Dwight Eddleman remain legendary. When Dike Eddleman sings the *Illinois Loyalty,* he gives new dimension to its meaning.

CHAPTER 12

HIS GREATEST CHALLENGE OF ALL

Throughout his six decades in the sports world, my father, Dike Eddleman, has proven to be a world-class competitor both on and off the playing field. Athlete. Executive. Husband. Father. Friend. Dike has excelled as all of these.

Associated with a Big Ten university the majority of those years, Dike stands apart from others as an icon of athleticism. To those who hold Illinois sports dear to their hearts, he seems to have been around forever. One cold morning in February 1995, this man who everyone thought might live forever proved he was merely mortal. Suffering a near-fatal heart attack, my father demonstrated that unique spirit and tenacity innate in his character. During his illness and recovery, he encountered the greatest challenge of his life.

Rarely does a person think about how drastically life can change overnight. My parents discovered they are no exception to this rule. Such a change occurred one morning while my mother prepared my father's breakfast. Dad came into the kitchen complaining that he felt hot and it was difficult for him to breathe. Alarmed by his symptoms, my mother insisted they immediately go to the emergency room at Carle Hospital. Little did either of them suspect what a profound effect that day would have on the rest of their lives.

After being examined in the emergency room and admitted to the cardiac unit, the Carle medical staff determined Dad needed triple-bypass surgery and a valve replacement. Because of his flu-like symptoms, the operation was postponed until his temperature and physical condition returned to normal. My brother, sisters and I were summoned home.

I will never forget the feeling of panic that shot through my body when I heard my mother's usually calm voice on the other end of the telephone. My mother always has been the rock of the family. Holding back the tears, I understood the urgency of her message and immediately rushed to Champaign.

My brother, Tom, and his wife, Lynn, had the shortest distance to travel from southwest Champaign. They were the first to arrive at the hospital. My younger sister, Kristy, was notified of Dad's illness in a timely fashion by Delta Airlines. Based in Cincinnati, she was flying a trip to Tampa. After landing in Tampa, she boarded the next plane headed north and arrived at Champaign's Willard Airport by 10:30 p.m. My sister, Nancy, was the most difficult to reach. After receiving word, she dropped her daughters off at a neighbor's house and caught the last flight of the day from San Antonio to Indianapolis.

By midnight, we were all gathered by our mother's side at our parents' home in Lincolnshire Fields. Informed of test results and the doctors' advice, the family prepared for what we thought would be routine heart surgery. Although it was a major operation, the family remained optimistic. We talked about the miracles of modern medicine and friends who had sailed through similar procedures. We were grateful for Dad's positive attitude. He hadn't been hospitalized since his knee surgery in high school! We settled in for the night, realizing many important decisions would be made in the days ahead.

At *1:30 a.m.*, the telephone rang with the ominous news that the trauma team had been called because Dad's condition was deteriorating rapidly. Mother was instructed to come to the hospital immediately. Emergency surgery was going to be performed as soon as possible.

The family arrived at Carle Hospital for a tedious 10-hour vigil. By 3 a.m. on February 26, 1995, the family had kissed its hero farewell and spoken words of encouragement as his gurney was pushed toward the operating room.

Dad hails from a healthy gene pool with ancestors who lived into their 80s and 90s, but this brought little comfort. We found ourselves feeling extremely uncomfortable in the hospital setting. The hours spent in the waiting room seemed endless. The prayers of ministers, calls from concerned friends and the presence of Dad's faithful secretary, Louita Hartwell, were appreciated, but they didn't make the waiting any easier.

My family kept in constant contact with the surgical team via the telephone. Just about the time Dad's surgery should have been completed, the phone rang and my mother answered it. Dad had suffered a massive heart attack on the operating table. Tears flowed, and my family prayed for Dad's life.

Echoes of grief broke the silence in the waiting room. We were all paralyzed with the fear of losing him. Nancy fell to her knees, clutched her chest and said, "Dear, God, NO!" Tom embraced my mother and his wife, Lynn. Kristy and Louita sobbed in each other's arms.

Roger Jenks, minister of the University Place Christian Church on Wright Street in Champaign, made a timely appearance. He arrived just seconds before my family received the surgical team's call. Reverend Jenks asked my mother if he could lead us in prayer. As hands were joined, I felt a sense of peace overcome the adrenaline rush that had caused my heart to race uncontrollably. "He's going to be all right. He's going to be all right." I repeated this over and over to myself. I prayed God's will be done.

There are angels on earth. My mother is one of the brightest and best. Another one is Matti Schmidt. I recall her greatest act of kindness during my father's ordeal. It was probably only

15 minutes between the time we got the call from the surgical team and Matti's entrance into the waiting room. Informed of the bleak news, Matti stood quietly patting my mother's shoulder.

Matti and my mother are made from the same mold. She is a woman of the '90s—intelligent, classy and a woman of action. I took Matti out into the hallway and said, "If something has happened to Dad, I want Mom to be with him." Matti, a Carle employee, found the nearest nurses' station and started dialing numbers. Almost instantly, Matti found out that Dad was out of the operating room and the cardiac surgeon's nurse was on her way to talk to us. Angels do the nicest things and their timing is perfect.

The news that Dad had survived gave us hope. When we were told he would be taken to the seventh-floor Intensive Care Unit, expressions of grief turned to tears of joy. The good news canceled the bad. What a fighter! Dad was *ALIVE!*

In the days, weeks and months ahead, my father's will to live was tenacious. Our celebration of his survival was premature, though. Dr. L. Scott Cook's nurse said Dad was in critical condition. He was kept comatose until his vital signs stabilized. Whatever transpired in the 48 hours after his surgery would be crucial. He was hooked up to a ventilator, a heart monitor and a myriad of other life support devices. That was the bad news. The good news was that my family could see him as often as the ICU staff allowed.

My mother and brother were the first to see Dad in ICU. When it was my turn to see him, I thought he looked wonderful, considering all he'd been through. He was tan from a recent trip to Acapulco. His face looked strong and healthy as if nothing traumatic had happened. Two at a time, we gently touched and embraced Dad for a few moments. Totally exhausted, my family and I left Carle counting our blessings and breathing sighs of relief. Thinking we were on the downhill side of this journey, we didn't realize the adventure was only beginning.

After the first few daily visits to Carle, each of us could have made the trip to the seventh floor blindfolded. Mother was determined to be with Dad from morning until night. Although we were concerned about *her* health and well-being, no one argued with her. Mom "worked" longer shifts than the nurses. She arrived at the hospital around 6 a.m. because that was the best time to talk to the physicians. She would stay until after 8 p.m. when the night shift came on duty.

Family members were given the ICU desk telephone number and told we could have a report on Dad's condition at any time. We soon developed special feelings for certain personnel who went above and beyond the call of duty. Mother recalled the kindness extended to her by hospital administrator Mike Fritz. So many calls came into the hospital that Mr. Fritz suggested Teddy should make a public statement about Dike's condition. University of Illinois Athletic Director Ron Guenther suggested that the calls be put through to the University of Illinois Division of Intercollegiate Athletics Office.

Because of the volume of calls during Dike's first week in the hospital, the athletic office had to assign one secretary whose only job was to answer calls about him. Inquiries came from everywhere, including Japan and Hawaii. From one end of the country to another, word of mouth spread the news. Concerned friends and colleagues cared enough to make visits or leave messages for the family. We were especially touched by the number of men who personally shared their sentiments. It was touching to see his friends displaying their emotions openly. Dr. John Pollard visited my father daily. "I wish you had come to see us sooner, my friend," the doctor told Dike in a soothing, sincere voice.

My family had high hopes for a routine recovery. It wasn't to be. Although my father always had a flair for performing well under pressure, his condition appeared to be deteriorating each day. The doctors said the serious infection Dad had when he entered the hospital was causing complications. Dr. Cook gave Mom the grim news that if the infection reached the new valve in Dad's heart, it might kill him. Percentages were given each day on his chances of survival. Despite the prognosis, no one gave up hope. Family members were tired and discouraged, but we knew if anyone could beat the odds, Dad would do it. He always had a way of winning the big ones.

As the days passed, Mom diligently continued her bedside vigil. Every day began with a prayer that the infection would respond to one of the new antibiotics. Then, Dad's breathing tube could be removed. Mom's greatest fear, at this point, was that Dad's larynx might be damaged permanently, causing him to lose the use of his vocal cords. Dad's doctors questioned Mom often, trying to pinpoint the cause of the infection. Had they been in the rural countryside in Mexico? During their vacation, had they been around strange animals? What kind of exotic foods had they eaten? The staff tested Dad for everything from Legionnaire's Disease to AIDS. Finally, after changing the antibiotic every few days, the infection began responding to one of the medications my father was being given intravenously. Dad had been in ICU for more than two weeks. He now had developed pneumonia.

Mom was extremely frustrated. When Dad would get past one hurdle, another would appear. My father always has been a survivor, and he was giving it his best effort. As the weeks passed, nerves frayed and days seemed endless. Stress was taking its toll on everyone, even Dad. One night, he looked up and tried to speak. His eyes filled with tears, and a few trickled down his cheeks. This was heartbreaking.

Despite my father's lack of improvement, my mother returned to the hospital each day with a renewed spirit. She checked on Dad and greeted the many friends who came to Carle to see her. She would position herself in the hallway on a blue love seat outside the ICU doors. Mom was given permission to see Dad at any time. She was grateful to the nursing staff for allowing her this privilege because it helped relieve some of her tension. Matti, Carle's resident angel, stopped by to see that my mother ate. At times, Matti got frustrated because Mom never wanted to leave her spot on that blue sofa.

My family watched other tragedies unfold. There was the death of a friend, Jack Walsh, whose large family befriended us. He had bypass surgery several days after Dad's. Jack's relatives summoned us to the telephone 20-30 times a day. The day Jack passed away, my family thought it had lost a comrade.

During the 28-day stint outside those ICU waiting-room doors, my family watched as one traumatized family after another came and went. Whether young or old, white or black, tragedy shows no mercy. It took our minds off of our problems to share someone else's. Some days our only diversion was learning that someone in ICU fought against greater odds than Dad. I recall looking out the windows by my father's bed and watching the world go along its merry way. I discovered firsthand how life support holds its victims in a state of cold and sterile apathy.

Since Dad had been bedridden for weeks, his nurses would sit him in a unique contraption that converted from a gurney into a chair. Although Dad was held upright by straps and belts, we thought he was conscious of his surroundings because he responded by nodding or gesturing. At times, Dad tried to talk despite his breathing tube. He had a television at the end of his bed. Mother would turn on his favorite programs like "Murder She Wrote," "60 Minutes," "Matlock," and "Perry Mason" re-runs or anything on ESPN.

By this time, March Madness had cast its spell over Illinois. Dad was going to miss attending the state basketball tournament for the first time since anyone could remember. We would read Loren Tate's *News-Gazette* sports column to him every evening. This evoked winks and nods from him which thrilled and encouraged us. Centralia had a good chance of playing in the state tournament in 1995. The team had asked if it could visit Dike if it made it to the Assembly Hall. Unfortunately, the Centralia Orphans lost at super-sectionals that year.

Dad does not remember much about ICU. He recalled having recurring dreams. He would be in different gyms like Centralia and Pontiac, and he always looked for my mother. Once, he thought Mom wanted to buy a new house. He recalled trying to tell her that he didn't want to move.

Occasionally, Dad asked for a pencil and paper. The first word or two was legible, but the rest would trail off to mere scribbled lines. It was frustrating for everyone.

By the third week in ICU, my father's lips were cracked and peeling. He seemed to relish eating a few ice chips. Dad had formed scabs on his face from the adhesive tape that held the breathing tube in place. His arms were full of bruises from the IVs that had been inserted. Because he was being fed only liquids through a tube in his nose, Dad was losing weight, too.

Despite his grave condition, sports always seemed to evoke a response. Dad would give us a thumbs up when we told him that Lou Tepper, Karol Kahrs, Itch Jones or Paula Smith had called or stopped by. Ron Guenther and Monsignor Duncan were two of his most frequent visitors. Ron extended every courtesy imaginable to my mother. It was the personal communication and precious time that Ron spent in that hallway outside ICU that revealed his character to my family. Ron Guenther is a loyal Illini who has shown great respect for Illinois and its many traditions.

Another Illini who showed his true colors was former basketball coach Lou Henson. Henson came to see Dad before leaving town for away games.

My father can recall only his last two weeks at Carle. One of the lowest points for my family was the day Dad's breathing tube was removed the first time. After several hours, Dad's breathing was labored and his blood pressure elevated. Having been told that the tube had been removed, I raced up to Carle after work to join in the celebration. The day we were waiting for finally had arrived! I met my brother, who said the tube had to be replaced. Sedated, Dad was doing fine. It was mother's state of mind that worried us. Having the tube reinserted was devastating to her morale.

My father's breathing tube *eventually* was removed. He was off the ventilator and breathing on his own! Those next 24 hours were torture. We stood beside Dad's bed with our eyes glued to the monitors. If his blood pressure and heart rate remained stable, he could be moved downstairs to the critical care floor! It was the first step closer to the front door. With more prayers, great medical care and mother's constant companionship, Dad soon was released from ICU.

When my father finally was placed on the rehab floor, his two goals were to gain back his strength and learn how to walk again. Dad admitted his greatest fear throughout his hospitalization was the possibility of not walking again. As usual, his tenacity and perseverance prevailed. It made his day when the staff gathered around the nurses' station and cheered as he shuffled by with his walker. He gained strength quickly after eating *real* food. My father has a passion for ice cream and was given this treat whenever he wanted it. Surprisingly, Dad lost only 25 pounds from his pre- to post-op weight check.

Dad referred to his physical therapy as boot camp. He hated it, but he worked hard because he wanted to go home. The day finally arrived when they put a calendar on his wall. On it was circled the tentative date when he might be released from the hospital. It was April 13, 1995, an anniversary date that he and my mother will long remember! To my father, who hadn't been sick a day in his adult life, his stay at Carle seemed like an eternity.

People react differently to stressful situations. Mother was strong and quiet during my father's ordeal. Tom found it painful to see Dad hooked up to all those infernal machines. My brother faithfully came to the hospital to be with Mom, but he looked pale as a ghost when he emerged from ICU. Tom and his wife, Lynn, never let Mom leave the hospital alone at night. Nancy spent most of her time patting Dad's arms and rubbing his shoulders, which drove my brother crazy. Kristy and I asked question after question of the medical team. There were seven different specialists treating him. Kristy was an excellent public relations representative. She did a wonderful job answering the telephone and updating everyone. We all contributed in our own way.

My mother and I enjoyed reading the 400 get-well cards and letters that my father received. The card that brought Dad the biggest smile was the 4' x 8' card that Tom Porter sent over from the University of Illinois Athletic Association. It was placed in the hospital's lobby for well-wishers to sign. It was filled in two weeks. The staff brought it to Dad's room in ICU. He still has it at home as a reminder of all the good wishes that were sent his way.

Dad was overwhelmed by all the prayers that were offered for him. He not only was remembered by his own congregation but also by many other churches around the state. Dozens of prayer cards were signed by strangers. This touched him deeply. Dad believes those prayers were a key to his recovery. Although my father gives credit to his physicians, family and friends for surviving those difficult 49 days, I believe it was his spirit and the heart of a true champion that allowed him to emerge the victor.

CONCLUSION

A LEGEND IS FOREVER

After his heart surgery, my father had a difficult time slowing down. My parents always have shared a "use it or lose it" attitude, especially in their later years. Dad made every attempt to follow doctors' orders. He wanted to get well. With the help of a cane, Dad soon was taking short walks around his neighborhood. His recovery had amazed everyone.

Scott Andresen, sportscaster for Champaign's WICD television station, put together a feature series about my Dad a month after his hospital release. The final segment announced the proclamation of yet another Dike Eddleman Day. This one was declared by Governor Jim Edgar on May 17, 1995, in Springfield.

This special recognition had been arranged by Republican Representative Ron Stephens and Senator Frank Watson of Southern Illinois. Senator Stan Weaver also was present at the ceremony, which took place at the State Capitol.

Immediate family members and close friends shared this special day with Teddy and Dike. Brent and Charlene Cain from Carlyle, Will and Marty Thomson from Galva, Guy and Brad Michael and Bob Baer from Highland watched the presentation in Springfield.

As I stood at the podium next to my mother and father that day, I thought that perhaps this honor was the most significant of all the accolades my father received. Looking back, Dad's survival was nothing short of a miracle. After his surgery, everyone in our family viewed each day as a precious gift.

John Avallone, director of the cardiac rehabilitation department at Carle Hospital, credits Dike's active lifestyle and exercise habits for providing the endurance and stamina from which he was able to draw throughout his surgery and recuperation. The lesson to be learned is that exercise should be a lifelong quest. Whatever activities people enjoy should be the ones they pursue to stay healthy and alert. John and Dike bonded during the cardiac exercise sessions that Dike participated in throughout late spring and early summer after his surgery. If it hadn't been for John's motivational sessions, Dad might not have been as quick to jump onto the treadmill or the exercise bike. After heart surgery, there are physiological and psychological changes with which a patient must deal. Although the pulleys, cranks and other exercise machines held little appeal for Dike, he knew John's advice was sound. The heart *is* a muscle. Muscles need exercise to stay strong. Once again, Dike accepted the challenge.

The great news is that Dike's perseverance once again paid off. On December 25, 1995, Teddy and Dike celebrated their golden wedding anniversary in San Antonio, Texas, where the whole family gathered for Christmas. The entire "Eddleman team," all 16 of them, including grandchildren, attended a romantic dinner on the Riverwalk to celebrate Dike and Teddy's 50 years together.

After dinner, their children gave them round-trip tickets to Hawaii, one of Teddy and Dike's favorite destinations. Why Hawaii? As you might imagine, there was an ulterior motive. The Illini basketball team was playing in the Rainbow Classic Tournament in Honolulu. Any time you combine sun, fun and the Orange and Blue, you're bound to find Teddy and Dike. They're still "loyal to you, Illinois" after all these years.

Five months and one day after celebrating Teddy and Dike's golden anniversary, I had the honor of being escorted down the aisle on the arm of my father to be joined in marriage to my former college sweetheart, Gene Lenzi. We had met on the University of Illinois campus as students in 1967. Having gone our separate ways, it was like a dream come true when we were reunited.

During the following Christmas holiday, Gene and I, along with our six children, joined Teddy and Dike aboard the Norwegian cruise ship the *M/S Dreamward*. While on board, Dike not only celebrated his 74th birthday, but my parents also celebrated their 51st wedding anniversary.

The future hopefully will hold more happy times and travels for Teddy and Dike. No one could ask for a lifetime of more thrilling memories together. There's an entire room full of photographs, trophies, medals and plaques in their home. Since I was young, I have been fascinated with my father's scrapbooks. As I studied pictures from the state tournament, the Rose Bowl, the Final Four and the Olympics, I could hear the cheering crowds. Even now when I sit in Dad's trophy room, I am in awe of his many accomplishments. As I touch his bronzed track shoes, I can only imagine the places they have been and the miles they have run. Recounting the lives of my parents has given me hours of enjoyment and a lesson in sports history. My father, Dike Eddleman, is a legend. With the trend toward specialization in sports, his story may never be equaled. It is a classic.

Blessed with the gifts of athletic talent and versatility *extraordinaire*, Dike's potential was noticed in the seventh grade when he high jumped 5-8 3/4 in his bare feet. Throughout his career, Dike continued to impress his audiences with performances in nearly every sport he played.

I hope it always will be remembered that in March 1942 one of the greatest high school basketball games of all time was played. Although there certainly have been higher-scoring games, perhaps there has never been a more exciting one. Out of Centralia, Illinois, one of the Southern hotbeds of basketball in the state at that time, came a premier athlete who sparked the imagination of every youngster from Chicago to Cairo.

A fine, young man, my father emerged from humble beginnings to become a superstar. Centralia became known as Eddlemanville, and his loyal fans called themselves Eddlemaniacs. He was indeed a phenomenon. In every sense, he was the personification of the heroic figure.

Boys wore rolled-up overalls because Dike wore his pants that way. Eddleman hunting caps and plaid jackets would sell out just as soon as they arrived at the local stores. Throngs of boys would mob him at the movie theater, his favorite place to go on Sunday afternoons, just for a chance to sit by their idol.

Throughout his high school career, fans would line up early waiting for Dike's bus to arrive so they could get a glimpse of the youthful legend. It was reported that at an away basketball game scheduled between the Centralia Orphans and the Taylorville Tornadoes, Taylorville fans began finding seats at 5:30 p.m. — 2 1/2 hours before tip-off time! One family even brought supper and ate it in the stands to be assured of a chance to watch Dike and the Orphans play basketball.

Autograph hounds approached him at every imaginable time and place. After scoring a record 969 points in basketball during his junior year in high school, Paramount Pictures approached his coach about making a movie of the 17-year-old sensation. "Coach Trout was sensible enough not to be taken in by the glamour of Hollywood," recalled Bill Davies, Eddleman's childhood friend and former high school teammate. "Besides, I'm sure it would have broken Illinois High School Association rules even back then. Not only did Dwight have great athletic ability, he was a real stud! He had it all!" After college, he was offered the leading role in a Tarzan movie.

In his quest for higher education, Eddleman chose to attend the University of Illinois (Champaign-Urbana), becoming the first member of his family to earn a college degree. He played on Illinois' 1947 Rose Bowl team and was captain of the 1948-49 Big Ten championship basketball team. That same year, he was selected the most valuable basketball player in the Big Nine. During the summer of his junior year at the University of Illinois, he won a berth on the United States Track and Field team and participated in the 1948 Olympics in London as one of the world's best high jumpers. As a Fighting Illini, he has the unequaled distinction of lettering 11 times in basketball, football and track. Adding those 11 monograms to the 12 he was awarded in high school, he earned enough letters to spell I·L·L·I·N·O·I·S' G·R·E·A·T·E·S·T A·T·H·L·E·T·E.

After college, he played professional basketball for the Tri-City Blackhawks, the Milwaukee Hawks and the Fort Wayne Zollner Pistons. After five successful seasons in the fledgling National Basketball Association, he took a job as personnel director for Central Soya Inc. In 1970, he became the executive director of the Fighting Illini Scholarship Fund at the University of Illinois, a position he held until January 1, 1993.

My father attributes his success to his family, friends and coaches. His half-sister became his legal guardian during high school, which allowed him to participate in sports at Centralia High School instead of moving to a rural town where he would have attended a one-room country school. His high school coach, Arthur L. Trout, taught him more than fundamentals. He taught him discipline, ethics and character. Eddleman always has been rich in friendships, remaining unpretentious throughout his years of athletic adventures.

Perhaps one of his greatest accomplishments in a gymnasium did not even involve athletics. During Dike's sophomore year in high school, a pretty, petite brunette who was walking through the gym on her way to class caught Eddleman's eye. The 5-foot-1 Teddy Georgia Townsley would become the high school sweetheart and the No. 1 fan of the 6-foot-3 Eddleman. On December 25, 1945, she became his wife after the couple exchanged wedding vows during a Christmas Day ceremony that took place while he was home on leave from the Army Air Corps.

Of all the factors contributing to Dike's success, it appears the most enduring influence has been his wife and best friend, Teddy. As a girl, she attended Irving Grade School but remembers watching the young Eddleman as he high-jumped on the playground at Central Grade School. As a Centralia High School cheerleader, she shared in the excitement of each victory and the disappointment of every defeat.

The words to Teddy and Dike's favorite song, "Someone to Watch Over Me," appear prophetic as they perfectly describe their marriage. Over the years, it has been a profoundly loving experience epitomized by common bonds that have solidified their relationship. The couple has shared a belief in God, a love for children, a zest for living and a passion for sports.

Their marriage resulted in the births of four children: three daughters and one son. Diana, Nancy, Tom and Kristy each attended the University of Illinois. The Eddleman children agree that their mother has provided an infinite source of strength and support for the family. Her dedication to her husband and children has been exemplary as she has touched their lives and their hearts by maintaining the highest standards and expectations.

From the early years to the present, my father remains a model of athletic excellence and spiritual integrity for both young and old alike. The trust he has earned from his friends and colleagues will be remembered as his outstanding legacy. As executive director of the Fighting Illini Scholarship Fund, he withstood the test of time, including NCAA investigations and retiring athletic directors, university presidents and head coaches.

The total monetary gifts to the Division of Intercollegiate Athletics of Illinois grew from about $145,000 annually in 1969 to more than $3,500,000 in 1992. Eddleman attributes the financial success of his department to a number of reasons. "I believe people trusted me with their donations. My program was always run with consistent policies and procedures. The money raised during my years at the University of Illinois came from one contributor at a time. I believed in my cause. I asked friends to help if they could. The response was very gratifying." Although his athletic achievements opened many doors for him, his sincerity and humility enhanced his career.

My father soared to athletic stardom in a simpler, more magical era. It was in the early 1940s, during those post-Depression and pre-war days, that his athletic career blossomed. With a basketball shooting style that was "more deadly than Clark Gable," he excelled when people were enchanted with their sports heroes. It long will be remembered that in Centralia, Illinois, an Orphan wearing jersey No. 40 became an idol to a town of worshiping fans. He was an inspiration to a generation of youngsters who rubbed their chins and noses raw shooting "Kiss Shots" to the stars trying to become the next Dike Eddleman. He carried this inspiration to a higher plateau in Champaign, Illinois, where he pursued an avocation that evoked his loyalty and devotion. It will be the difficult task of those who follow him to live up to the standards of dedication and integrity that have been established by Dike during a time that long will be remembered as the Eddleman Era.

Other University of Illinois titles published by Sports Publishing Inc., include:

Illini Legends, Lists, and Lore: 100 Years of Big Ten Heritage
by Mike Pearson

Grange, Butkus, Virgin, Henson, Huff, Zuppke, Battle, Boudreau, Eddleman, Eggers, Buford, and Howard - these are some of the greatest collegiate athletes, not only at Illinois, but throughout the country. *Illini Legends, Lists, and Lore: 100 Years of Big Ten Heritage* is the first book to capture the history of all sports at Illinois.
ISBN 1-57167-010-6 • $29.95 • 212 pp

The Big Ten: A Century of Excellence
by Dale Ratermann

The Big Ten: A Century of Excellence is the definitive history of intercollegiate athletics' oldest and most prestigious conference. Designed in an easy-to-read format, the Conference-endorsed Big Ten centennial book contains pages of historical reference material about the league's first 100 seasons. Among the features included in each of the four-page chapters are sketches of the big events, features on the team champions, stories about the premier athletes, notes about the influential coaches and administrators, information about the Big Ten's pioneers, and vignettes about the Conference's academic achievements. The book's appendix includes a synopsis of each university's coaches and administrators.
ISBN 1-57167-037-8 • $39.95 • 456 pp

Lou: Winning at Illinois
by Lou Henson and Skip Mylenski

"...Lou has brought loads of excitement to the Fighting Illini program and prestige to the Big Ten."   -Dick Vitale, *ABC Sports*

Follow Coach Henson's career and trip to the Final Four in Seattle. *Lou: Winning at Illinois* provides an inside look at the normally private Henson and the program he headed.
ISBN 0-915611-24-4 • $18.95 • 266 pp

Ray Eliot: The Spirit and Legend of Mr. Illini
by Doug Cartland

Ray Eliot spent 18 years as head coach of the Fighting Illini. Eliot led Illinois to three Big Ten titles and two Rose Bowl championships in eight years. He was voted National Coach of the Year by the Los Angeles Times in 1951. Eliot's devotion to young men and old-fashioned loyalty to the University of Illinois set him apart and created the legendary mystique of "Mr. Illini."
ISBN 1-57167-015-7 • $19.95 • 250 pp

Hail to the Orange and Blue: 100 Years of Illinois Football Tradition
by Linda Young

This book details the history of Illinois football with more than 200 photographs. Some famous events featured include: Bob Zuppke's elevation from high school coach to architect of national powerhouses; Harold "Red" Grange's touchdown gallops in the sparkling new Memorial Stadium; Julius Rykovich's 98-yard interception return in 1946; the 1951, 1960, and 1983 Rose Bowl seasons; and much more.

ISBN 0-915611-31-7 • $29.95 • 246 pp

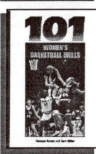

The Fire Still Burns
by Mike Hebert with Dave Johnson

As one of the nation's most successful collegiate coaches in any sport, Mike Hebert took the coaching road less traveled with astonishing results. In his 10 years with the University of Illinois, Hebert transformed an ignored women's volleyball program into the hottest ticket in town.

ISBN 0-915611-77-5 • $19.95 • 184 pp

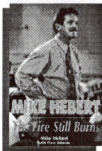

101 Women's Basketball Drills
by Theresa Grentz

Nationally recognized coach of the University of Illinois' women's basketball team, Theresa Grentz presents her top 101 basketball drills that have helped her develop championship quality players and teams.

ISBN 1-57167-083-1 • $15.00 • 127 pp

The Magic of Medicare 7, 8 or 9 and All That Jazz
by Nancy Gilmore

The Dixieland jazz group Medicare 7, 8 or 9 is unique in University of Illinois history. Originally consisting mainly of gray-haired faculty members, the band gave what it thought was its first and only performance in 1969 as a "peace offering" to help ease the tension so prevalent on college campuses throughout the country during the Vietnam era. Twenty-seven years later, with thousands of performances under its belt, and a roster of nearly 135 alumni musicians, the band, and the beat go on.

ISBN 0-915611-75-9 • $19.95 • 134 pp

────── *Available in all fine bookstores* ──────

or to order any of these titles *call* 1(800)327-5557, *fax* (217)359-5975, *e-mail* us at books@sagamorepub.com or *send* orders to Sports Publishing Inc., 804 North Neil Street, Suite 100, Champaign, IL 61820.